THE FILMS OF SHIRLEY TEMPLE

ALSO BY ROBERT WINDELER

Julie Andrews
Sweetheart: The Story of Mary Pickford
Shirley Temple

THE FILMS OF
SHIRLEY
TEMPLE

By ROBERT WINDELER

CITADEL PRESS   SECAUCUS, N.J.

First edition
Copyright © 1978 by Robert Windeler
All rights reserved
Published by Citadel Press
A division of Lyle Stuart Inc.
120 Enterprise Ave., Secaucus, N. J. 07094
In Canada: George J. McLeod Limited, Toronto
Manufactured in the United States of America by
Halliday Lithograph, West Hanover, Mass.
Designed by A. Christopher Simon

Library of Congress Cataloging in Publication Data
Windeler, Robert.
  The films of Shirley Temple.

   1. Temple, Shirley, 1928-   2. Moving-
picture actors and actresses—United States—
Biography. I. Title
PN2287.T33W48   791.43'028'0924 [B] 78-1408
ISBN 0-8065-0615-6

For Those Artists and Entertainers
Who Also Work Hard
to Make a Better World

ACKNOWLEDGMENTS

Many individuals were helpful to me in the researching of this book, and I'm particularly grateful to Allan Dwan, Buddy Ebsen, former Senator George Murphy, the late Robert Graham Paris, and Jane Withers for their memories of Little Shirley. Jim Eason of KSO-FM in San Francisco and Lisa Trumpler of the German magazine *Brigitte* helped to capture her as an adult on tape and were generous with their transcripts. Thanks also to Barbara Baker, who assisted in the selection of photographs, and Judith Young and Merle Freeman, who made the manuscript look good.

CONTENTS

THE FILMS OF SHIRLEY TEMPLE

The best-known face of the mid 1930s, not excluding FDR's.

INTRODUCTION

Without possibility of argument she was the most famous child in the world. The image of her very public childhood belongs to the ages, although she never made a single motion picture that she or anybody else thought was really any good. Starting in movies at the age of three, Shirley Temple was just playing games, and so, in a sense, were the tens of millions in her audience. The chief game was called "Beat the Depression" (a harsh reality never visible in any of Shirley's fantastical films), and more than any other person, she did just that—at least according to Franklin D. Roosevelt, who presided over the United States of America for all the years she was a child star.

In the 1930s, six-year-olds of all ages made Shirley Temple box-office queen of the world for a record four years running, when she was aged seven to ten (although her parents and the studio lied that she was six to nine). She was *Time*'s "cinemoppet," and the youngest person ever to appear on the magazine's cover; the youngest person ever listed in *Who's Who*; and the youngest ever to get an Academy Award.

Not only was she a kind of midget folk heroine, she was also an attraction for the world's great, who also beat a path to her dressing room door. Eleanor Roosevelt, Noel Coward, J. Edgar Hoover and Thomas Mann left the soundstages of 20th Century-Fox (as all her prominent visitors did) proudly wearing a Shirley Temple Police Force badge. Her official eighth birthday (really her ninth) brought more than 135,000 presents from around the world, including a baby kangaroo from Australia and a prize Jersey calf from a class of school-children in Oregon. In 1938 her income was the seventh highest in America (the top six were industrialists, including MGM's Louis B. Mayer), at $307,014, and that was just before she started earning $300,000 per picture, and making three or four a year.

Others had paved the way for the possibility of a Shirley Temple. Principally, they were Mary Pickford (who, while in her twenties and thirties, played children of ten or twelve in silent features), Jackie Coogan (who played *The Kid* with Charlie Chaplin in 1920, and *Peck's Bad Boy* and *Oliver Twist*), and Hal Roach, with his "Our Gang" series beginning in 1921. But they had worked their magic in combinations of drama, melodrama and mayhem in silent movies. Shirley was born in 1928, the year sound films really took over, and she made her first one-reelers in 1932, the year Pickford retired. Shirley had a brand new medium in which both more and less were required of a child. There was less acting, certainly, but more singing, dancing, shaking the finger, bowing the mouth to actually say something—like "oh, my goodness"—and, above all, dimpling. And no one did any of those things better or more appealingly than Shirley.

The child stars who came after her were different too. Mickey Rooney and Judy Garland were really adolescents with other kinds of situations in their films, and Judy's musicals—albeit escapist—had more lasting merit than Shirley's and were made in Technicolor, something Shirley experienced only briefly. Tiny Margaret O'Brien in the 1940s was more of an actress than Shirley, and at her most brilliant in scary circumstances. World War II brought more serious subject matter to films. As realism overtook fantasy in the movies in the 1950s there was no longer a place for child stars. Brandon de Wilde and Hayley Mills were the two exceptions in the 1950s and 1960s. In 1974 ten-year-old Tatum O'Neal won an Oscar as the con-child in *Paper Moon*. But as Buddy Ebsen, Shirley's dancing partner in 1936's *Captain January* groused, "That's no child, that's a hoodlum. Where did they go?"

Where indeed. But while she lasted, little Shirley Temple was an original. As Bill "Bojangles" Robinson, her most famous dancing partner, put it: "God made her just all by herself—no series, just one." When she got to be a gangly thirteen-year-old, Shirley wisely retired from movies, to go to school for the first time. She came back with limited success for a series of roles as a teenager, and quit the film world for good in 1949. She was twenty-one, just at the age most people start working for a living, and her self-earned fortune of between three and four million dollars was intact.

At that age she had already survived her young marriage to John Agar, and the divorce from him that had created the only scandal of her life. She was the mother of a year-old daughter and ready to try marriage and motherhood all over again. More importantly, she survived the whole of her early life and emerged as a sane and contributing human being. Whatever reservations others may have had about Shirley Temple as an adult, she herself had none.

Jackie Coogan had had to sue his mother and

Even at 18 months Shirley flashed the dimples and the smile that were to become famous the world over; her mother already harbored dreams of show business success for her.

Shirley and her mother Gertrude were nearly insepararable; Gertrude was Shirley's dialogue coach, wardrobe mistress and intermediary between directors and star, as well as a mom determined her daughter wouldn't be spoiled.

14

stepfather to recover even a small percentage of the four million dollars he earned as a child (thereby inspiring the state of California's "Coogan Law," which protected Shirley, and those who followed, from grasping guardians). Shirley's father, on the other hand, was a banker who invested her earnings wisely and mostly on her behalf. Other former child stars, unable to cope with growing up or suddenly not being adored by millions, retreated to alcohol, multiple marriages, dope and pills. A few kept trying to get work as actors, since acting was the only thing they knew how to do.

Still others got as far away from Hollywood as fast as they could. English-born Freddie Bartholomew, most famous for the talkie remake of *Little Lord Fauntleroy* and *David Copperfield*, became an advertising executive on New York's Madison Avenue. Canada's Deanna Durbin, after a decade of Hollywood stardom, mostly in musicals, turned her back so firmly on the fame and glamour of her former profession that she refused even to talk about it. In anonymity, she later lived in a small village an hour outside Paris, with her husband and two children. Villagers knew her only as Madame David and acted to protect her privacy. Someone from a garage opposite her farmhouse warned her of unfamiliar visitors if they approached, and she never answered the door or telephone herself.

Margaret O'Brien, the biggest child star of the 1940s, earned an Academy Award at eight, $2,500 a week at nine, and top-ten box-office ranking both years, in 1944 and 1945. Although she had to make some severe adjustments to young adulthood, Margaret never regretted her childhood, and continued in an acting career, mostly on television, in the 1960s and 1970s. Dean Stockwell, *The Boy with Green Hair*, and star of *Gentleman's Agreement*, was outspoken in his bitterness. "It's a miserable way to bring up a child," he said. "The life of a child star frustrates normal interests and associations with other children. I had no friends except my brother and I never did what I wanted to do. I had one vacation in nine years."

Shirley Temple had none of these problems or adjustments. After her divorce from John Agar and a happy second marriage to Charles Black, she left Hollywood and found a new life in other worlds: Washington, D.C., northern California, New York City, and Ghana. She raised two more children and returned to her hometown only intermittently in the late 1950s and early 1960s for television work, always staying in hotels and leaving the minute the work was over. Living down her former self was not a problem for her "within my circle of friends or really with anyone except a few middle-aged people who are stuck on this image of the little girl," she said just before going to Africa in 1974 to be United States Ambassador to Ghana. "That's their problem."

She made a clear distinction between herself and that screen character of over thirty-five years ago: "I have always thought of her as 'the little girl.' I never had a sister and she's sort of like that. She's opened up a lot of doors for me because she's known all over the world and that's a big advantage for me. I know her well and I even remember some of the dance routines she did, but she's not me."

Twenty-five years of volunteer work, local and national Republican politics, work at the United Nations and on problems of the environment led Mrs. Black to prominence in diplomatic circles. Misfortune struck in late 1972, in the form of breast cancer, but Shirley became the first public figure to make her mastectomy public to help those similarly afflicted and got more than 50,000 letters praising her action. It was only a temporary setback.

In the late 1970s, the scrapbooks of her show business career lined the shelves of the library in her large Tudor home in Woodside, California·(a suburb south of San Francisco that someone once called a hotbed of social rest), and prints of her movies were in the toolshed. Shirley Temple Black herself was in Ghana and Washington, not only living in the world, but trying hard to make it better.

While hopeful stage mothers and their progeny from all sections of the United States and Canada descended on Hollywood at an estimated rate of 400 a day in the 1930s, ironically, most of the little boys and girls who made it big in the movies were native Californians, starting with Los Angeles-born Jackie Coogan. Perhaps this was because they were brought up less frenzied about the show side of show business (and more canny about the business side), or simply because they were in exactly the right place at exactly the right time. Whatever the reason, the biggest child star of all was no exception to the rule. Shirley Jane

Baby Burlesks co-stars, out of diapers and into street clothes, pose for a candy bar promotion, which helped to finance the one-reelers.

Even during her early "loan-out" days at Paramount Shirley was lording it over other child actors—in this case Baby Leroy.

Temple was born at 9 P.M., April 23, 1928, at Santa Monica Hospital in Santa Monica, a small city on the Pacific Ocean a scant dozen miles west of Hollywood.

"Long before she was born I tried to influence her future life by association with music, art and natural beauty," her mother, Gertrude Temple, said in 1934. "Perhaps this prenatal preparation helped make Shirley what she is." Nothing else in Shirley's parents' background accounted for her career, except that Gertrude herself had wanted to act. But instead, this daughter of a Chicago jeweler had attended Polytechnic High School in Los Angeles and met and married George Temple when she was only seventeen. He had been born in Fairview, Pennsylvania, of Pennsylvania Dutch parentage and arrived in Los Angeles as a child in 1903. Although his family specialized in producing doctors, he opted for banking. When Shirley was born the Temples owned a one-story stucco house in Santa Monica, and a small LaSalle sedan. They had two sons, Jack and George, Jr., who were twelve and seven at the time of Shirley's birth.

"My mother was kind of afraid to have a third child," Shirley recalled, "because she wanted a girl but she was afraid she would have another boy. So my dad went to the family doctor, and he said, 'if you have your tonsils out, you will have a girl.' So they removed my dad's tonsils, and they grew back. He had to have them out a second time, and nine months after the second operation I was born. There is no medical reason for this story, but I think it's funny, and so I wanted to tell it, even though it always makes my parents angry."

Shirley walked at thirteen months, and when she was two, according to her mother, "she began to display a rare sense of rhythm and would keep time with her feet to the music on the radio." When Shirley was three Gertrude wanted to enroll her in a professional dancing class for children whose parents entertained screen ambitions for them. George only very reluctantly agreed. (He was a young banker with three children, this was the Depression, the bank had already closed several times, there had been wholesale pay cuts and fifty cents a week for dance lessons was a lot in 1931.) While Shirley quickly became the baby star pupil of her class at Meglin Dancing School, it wasn't the lessons, according to Mrs. Temple, that could "be credited with developing Shirley's personality. That is something she always had."

Just as stage mothers hounded them, movie talent scouts regularly scoured dancing and singing schools for children, hoping to pick up a prodigy for a modest salary. Charles Lamont, a director at Educational Studios, was on the prowl for precocious tots not more than three feet high. The day he arrived at Shirley's school she was underdressed for the rainy day. (Mrs. Temple was apparently the only mom who didn't know of the talent search; the other girls were in their Sunday best.) "I hid under the piano," Shirley recalled. "Obviously no poise. He stood around for a while watching, and then he said, 'I'll take the one under the piano.'"

Still two years in age away from kindergarten, to which she would never get, Shirley was signed on at Educational at ten dollars a day to appear in a series of one-reel Baby Burlesks, takeoffs on adult movies and stars. She graduated to two-reelers for Educational, "Frolics of Youth," at fifteen dollars a day. Producer Jack Hays signed her to a contract at fifty dollars per picture, to which he tried to hold her after she left and signed with 20th Century-Fox. In court Hays produced a contract giving him exclusive rights to Shirley Temple's services, but it was signed only in

Shirley also liked to get involved in some of the more peripheral moviemaking jobs; here she helps to unload caterer's lunches on an out-of-town location, 1934.

Some of Shirley's dogs were camera shy, but most took after her.

17

Whomping James Dunn at checkers was a favorite pasttime on the set.

James Dunn read to Shirley from books like *Silly Symphonies*, but she didn't necessarily hang onto every word.

LETTERS

To My Valentine

FOR MY

VALENTINE

In 1934 director David Butler at(230 pounds) and the star of *Bright Eyes* (45 pounds) were Valentines—at least in this studio publicity shot.

her childish scrawl and was thrown out by the judge.

Gertrude had hustled Shirley around to the studios, encouraged by her success at Educational and fueled with ambition for her daughter. George's position at the bank had improved, so the money was now secondary. Shirley had been rejected along with thousands of others by Hal Roach for the "Our Gang" comedies, and by Fox and most of the other studios. She managed a few small roles in major productions, but thankfully there were always the "Frolics of Youth" to fall back on. In 1932 Shirley did a bit part in her first full-length feature, *The Red-Haired Alibi*.

Billed as Shirley Jane Temple, in 1933 she did

a small role in a Zane Grey western starring Randolph Scott, *To the Last Man*. *Out All Night* the same year gave her the chance to work with one of Mary Pickford's old directors, Sam Taylor, and ZaSu Pitts, who predicted greatness for the child. Shirley made a musical with Janet Gaynor, Lionel Barrymore and Robert Young, but her part was too small for her to have a song, and did another bit in *Mandalay*, a Kay Francis vehicle. But no one except Miss Pitts had yet singled her out as anything more remarkable than just another cute kid.

It was one of her "Frolics of Youth," entitled *Pardon My Pups*, that led to Shirley Temple's real breakthrough. At a Beverly Hills preview of the two-reeler, songwriter Jay Gorney was struck by her work and asked Gertrude to have Shirley audition for his partner Lew Brown for a specialty number at the end of a feature at first called *Fox Follies*, then renamed *Stand Up and Cheer*. After hearing almost two hundred other applicants, Brown (who had also given Jackie Cooper his big movie break) gave Shirley the job the moment she finished singing the song, "Baby, Take a Bow." Her vaudeville number with James Dunn was the very last in the film, and she quite simply stole the picture, even causing most reviewers, who had dozed off, to revive.

Even before the release of *Stand Up and Cheer*, Winfield Sheehan, Fox's vice-president of production, who (along with everyone else who had witnessed her musical "debut" during the filming) was captivated by Shirley's talent, tied her up with a seven-year contract at $150 weekly. Before she was six, and even at this relatively modest salary for movies, Shirley was already outearning her father. Although Shirley was actually six in April of 1934, the Temples and the studio conspired to subtract a year from her age, to prolong her kiddie career and make her seem even more precocious than she was. All official biographical material on Shirley was issued with April 23, 1929, as her birth date, and a faked birth certificate with that date was printed up. It was only when she was "twelve" (actually thirteen) that Shirley herself found out—along wih the rest of the world—how old she really was.

Both the song "Baby, Take a Bow," and the movie, *Stand Up and Cheer*, were hits on release in early 1934, and she was the only thing novel about the picture. Newspapers ran still photographs of Shirley from it in favor of those of the stars. Exhibitors began billing the film "Shirley

She always liked uniforms and costumes, but sometimes her cowboy boots pinched.

Ducks were especially desirable for Easter publicity pictures, but Shirley liked all animals.

19

Her pets were always welcome on the set, no matter what else was going on.

orphan who reforms bookie Sorrowful Jones (Adolphe Menjou, who was equally memorable). "No more engaging child has been beheld on the screen," wrote the *New York Times* critic Mordaunt Hall on the release of *Little Miss Marker*, in May of 1934.

Until she saw herself on the screen for the first time in *Little Miss Marker*, Shirley had seen only one movie, *Skippy*, starring Jackie Cooper. She liked herself in the film, and applauded often during the preview. The reviews of *Little Miss Marker* were read to her, but the fan mail most carefully was not, since almost all of it said things like "I think you are the most beautiful baby in the world."

After her second film at Paramount, *Now and Forever*, with Carole Lombard and Gary Cooper, Shirley returned to Fox for minor roles in *Now I'll Tell*, with Spencer Tracy and Alice Faye and *Change of Heart*, a Janet Gaynor–Charles Farrell vehicle. Spurred on by the million-dollar gross their rival studio had reaped on *Little Miss Marker*, Fox now made *Baby, Take a Bow*, borrowing the song title and giving Shirley star billing, but below the title.

"I was really a fortunate person to be in movies at that time," Shirley remembered. "I had a lot of fun, caused a lot of trouble. I was a tomboy, although no one really knew that because they always saw me in the nice little dresses, and gloves. I really wanted to be a G-woman . . . or a vegetable salesman, or a pie salesman. Then when I became a teenager I got a little more class and decided I wanted to be a brain surgeon, but I figured no one would come to me. I never really wanted to be an actress. I just enjoyed all of this because when you start anything at age three, you don't realize it is work."

Gertrude, while dedicated to Shirley's career, was more unassuming and less pushy than most of her rival stage mothers. "I had a very shy mother, and she is still a very shy mother," Shirley said shortly before Gertrude and George celebrated their sixtieth wedding anniversary at the end of 1974. "My mother made all of our clothes and was a real homemaker. I think she first sent me to dancing school to get me out of the house. She was the only one who ever spanked me and she only spanked me once. I was very firm-skinned—and I still am—and I broke the ruler she used on the first swat."

Temple in *Stand Up and Cheer*" even though the studio's official credits had her way down the list, lumped with others in specialty numbers. The fan mail for her began to come in at a relative trickle, twenty or thirty letters a day. Then it jumped to two hundred, then five hundred.

Shirley was clearly a star, but Hollywood still distrusted its children. Other actors didn't like to play with them; some grownups wouldn't pay to see them; they were a nuisance on the set, temperamental and hard to teach. Fox, not quite knowing how to deal with her, let Shirley go to Paramount on loanout for two movies. In the first, *Little Miss Marker*, she played the memorable title role in Damon Runyon's story, the

This angel face won hundreds of millions of film-goers' hearts worldwide and helped make Shirley box-office champ in 1935.

Looking apprehensively at the chimney, Shirley isn't sure Santa Claus can squeeze through.

Carpenters, prop men, electricians and other workers on *Bright Eyes* bought Shirley some early Christmas presents, to keep her occupied when she wasn't on camera.

Her miniature special Academy Award for 1934 was presented by humorist Irvin S. Cobb at a banquet early in 1935.

Mrs. Temple had been concerned that in *Little Miss Marker* Shirley had hung out with gangsters and said things like "Aw nuts." She was assured that after *Baby, Take a Bow* Shirley's screenplays would be "more suitable to her cheery personality." And for the rest of the 1930s they were tailor-made to Miss Temple's image, if not to Miss Temple. Father George continued to oversee the family finances—including Shirley's. "I never cared about money when I was little," Shirley said.

George Temple was short, very stocky, with protruding pot and posterior, thinning dark hair and brown eyes, a snub nose and the dimples of his daughter. He invariably dressed in a gray suit off the rack. His wife was good-looking, taller than he, with olive skin, high cheekbones and an affable large mouth that spoke in a rather flat voice. Her regular, slightly hard features were well preserved, and she took good care of herself and her face. She looked nothing like Shirley, which led to outrageous propositions to George from women who wanted a daughter like Shirley. "My parents didn't smoke or drink," said Shirley, "and never went to Hollywood parties."

By the summer of 1934 six-year-old Shirley Temple was established as a full-fledged movie star. Her contract with the newly amalgamated 20th Century-Fox was adjusted—mostly at the instigation of her banker father—and her weekly salary leaped from $150 to $1,000. In addition, the new agreement provided a clutch of dolls and a Shetland pony for Shirley, as well as "comfortable and exclusive dressing room facilities," and a $250 weekly salary for Mrs. Gertrude Temple. The contract, at Mama's insistence, called for Shirley to be barred from the studio's commissary to prevent her being "petted and pampered."

A ten-room bungalow "dressing room" was converted to a kiddie-cozy home for Shirley, but for a few weeks she had to violate her new contract by eating at the Fox commissary because she couldn't get into her bungalow until Gloria Swanson, in temporary residence, moved out. There was also a clause in the new Temple contract to the effect that if Shirley's parents felt her screen work was changing her personality or keeping her from a normal girlhood they could break the contract and retire their daughter. "We'd do so, too," Mrs. Temple assured the press.

With her sons away at school, Jack at Stanford and George, Jr., at New Mexico Military Institute,

You can see why her mother called her "Presh."

23

Will Rogers and Shirley Temple were among the most popular movie stars in the world in 1934, a year before his death.

"Daddy's home from the bank!" Santa Monica, 1935.

Shirley liked young men in uniform, even Eagle Scouts—twenty-five of them from Southern California were honored by her at a luncheon also attended by Mrs. Frank Merriam, wife of the state's governor.

Postmaster General James Farley and Shirley pose at sea, 1935.

Between takes Shirley sat in her bungalow dressing room and read or studied—when she wasn't playing games.

Shirley liked to read her reviews, even in Swedish.

25

Gertrude was able to devote all of her time to Shirley, and she never left the child's side at work, and seldom after hours. Officially Gertrude was paid her Fox salary (later raised to $500 a week) to manage, dress and chaperone Shirley, and certainly to keep the golden curls in order. Unofficially, Mother Temple was the go-between for director and child star, and she was expected to keep Shirley unspoiled and from getting too far ahead in her education. By strictly forbidding advanced books and most outside influences, Shirley's parents held her back to the point that when she took a Pitner-Cunningham I.Q. test at the University of California at Los Angeles, Shirley, aged seven years, three months, tested only at nine years, seven months, despite an obvious and demonstrated precocity that was expected to merit an eleven-year-old's rating.

With regular work—she made no fewer than eight movies in 1934—Shirley's life began to take on a regular rhythm. She awoke each morning at seven, was given a glass of orange juice and then lay in bed for forty-five minutes, going over her lines and rehearsing dance steps lying on her back and waving her little legs in the air. After a breakfast of stewed fruit (her favorite was canned pears), one soft-boiled egg from the bantam chickens she kept at the studio, and bacon or cereal on alternate mornings, she and her mother went to the studio in their modest LaSalle, arriving at 9 A.M. for school even on mornings when there was no Temple film shooting.

Shirley had a standard public school desk in her bungalow and used California-issued textbooks, returning them to the state at the end of the year. Miss Frances Klampt ("Klammie"), under the supervision of the Los Angeles School Board of Education, taught Shirley the regular public school curriculum (complete with yearly examinations) and also served as a social service worker, overseeing Shirley's daily working conditions. During the filming of a picture, Shirley took her lessons between scenes in the morning and took three hours for lessons in the afternoon.

Her lunch hour was just exactly that, in her bungalow, and she ate her biggest meal of the day, although supper at home at six was a hefty soup, salad, three vegetables, a small amount of meat and a light pudding. After playing with her father and rehearsing her lines and routines with her mother for the next day, Shirley went to bed. Her friends were carefully selected from among

her neighbors and contemporaries, and their parents were requested not to take the children to Shirley's movies lest they get the idea that she was something special. However, her stand-in at the studio was Mary Lou Islieb, a neighbor and the daughter of a branch bank manager who had worked with Mr. Temple.

At the studio Shirley was maternal toward her bantam chickens, a dozen rabbits and dolls from all over the world dressed in native costume. And while she was not prone to cry when she hurt herself, she burst into an almost hysterical fit of sobbing when her favorite doll's arm fell off. She in turn was tractable to direction and instinctively obedient to the wishes of adults. The usually well-behaved, obsessively cheerful and optimistic Shirley Temple that her hordes of adoring fans saw on screen was the Shirley Temple behind the scenes as well, bright and lively, stopping just short of sass. A friend introduced H. G. Wells to Shirley on the set, saying, "He is the most important man in the Universe"; Shirley contradicted with "Oh, no, the most important one is God and Governor Merriam is second."

Bright Eyes, Shirley's last movie in 1934, and the first in a long string of Shirley Temple Christmas (and Easter) pictures, was a landmark film for her in many ways. Her billing was raised to above the title.

SHIRLEY TEMPLE
in
BRIGHT EYES

In the movie she sang what is probably the closest thing she had to a theme song: "On the Good Ship Lollipop."

Bright Eyes also made financial history for Fox. It cost $190,000 to produce and made back its negative cost in just three weeks of first-run engagements. Shirley's fan mail soared to 2,500 letter per week. *Bright Eyes* and her seven other films in 1934 put Shirley in eighth place in the *Motion Picture Herald*'s box-office poll of exhibitors for the year, behind Will Rogers, Clark Gable, Janet Gaynor, Wallace Beery, Mae West, Joan Crawford and Bing Crosby. (In 1935, 1936, 1937 and 1938 Shirley topped the *Motion Picture Herald* poll, the only star ever to do it four years in a row.) The studio insured her for $25,000 with Lloyds of London—because United States companies refused, on the grounds of age. Lloyds did

Never really having time to do her own housework, Shirley was nonetheless a symbol of child industry and helpfulness.

By example Shirley got her contemporaries into proper raingear.

At age six, Shirley sat very still, posed in a replica of the painting "Her First Sermon," which was painted in 1863 by Sir J. E. Millais.

insist as a condition of the insurance (and with a straight face) that Shirley not take up arms in warfare or join the army in peacetime; the insurance would be voided if the six-year-old died or was injured while intoxicated.

In February of 1935, at the annual banquet of the Academy of Motion Picture Arts and Sciences, Shirley was awarded an honorary gold statuette for 1934 for having "achieved eminence among the greatest of screen actors." The citations that went with her Oscar read, "There was one great towering figure in the cinema game in 1934, one artiste among artists, one giant among troupers. The award is bestowed because Shirley Temple brought more happiness to millions of children

and millions of grown-ups than any child of her years in the history of the world." Even at that time Shirley had some perspective on the situation, and she put the Oscar with her other dolls. And in later years she was the first to admit that acting had nothing to do with it.

"What are we going to pretend today?" little Shirley would ask her mother and the director, in that order. "She didn't act or make pictures," said David Butler, director of *Bright Eyes*, *The Little Colonel*, *The Littlest Rebel* and *Captain January*. "She played wonderful games. She got into fairyland, she believed it all herself and that's why you believed it."

At first Shirley tended to confuse her scripts with reality. During the filming of *Our Little Girl* early in 1935 she had to say to Lyle Talbot in one scene, "And anyway I don't like you." As soon as the scene was shot Shirley went over to Talbot and said solemnly, "I'm sorry Mr. Talbot, but those lines are in the script; I really do like you."

But with each picture her camera technique improved. The simple scenes were pure play, no more tiring than dressing her dolls and not so exhausting as a game of hide-and-seek. And if a director about to shoot an over-the-shoulder close-up said, "Now, Shirley . . ." she would get annoyed with herself and interrupt him with "You want me to be here, don't you?" and move so that her head was in full frame instead of slightly blocked by the other actor's chin or cheek.

Shirley always knew when she had made a mistake in the middle of a difficult scene or a complicated dance routine and would hold up her little hand to spoil the take so that a new one would have to be started, pre-empting, like many later actresses, the director's prerogative to yell "cut." She wasn't overly sensitive to criticism. "You can do lots better than that," director Butler told her after a scene in *Captain January*. Shirley winked, as she had seen her older colleagues do and said, "There was a little faking in it."

In singing silently to her own playback (moving her lips while a recording machine played a record already prepared by her of the tune she was singing for the camera), she achieved an uncanny perfection and always looked as if she were singing the tune on screen. Her lips were never out of "sync." Incredibly, she did many times what few other singers on the screen have done once—

Walt Disney won a special Oscar for *Snow White and the Seven Dwarfs,* his first feature-length animation, and Shirley presented it and seven "dwarf" oscars at the Academy Awards of 1938.

made a perfectly synchronized playback in the first take.

Her association with the sharper show business men and women she met at work, most of whom took a special interest in her, gave Shirley at ages six, seven and eight the professionalism, easy repartee and love of catch phrases of a seasoned trouper. She whooped with delight when her mentor and favorite dancing partner, Bill (Bojangles) Robinson, told her the old vaudeville wheeze, "How's the tailoring business?"—"So-so."

When she sat down to play her favorite game of squares, she'd often say, "There aren't any spots on your suit but you're going to the cleaners." Her precocity annoyed Dr. Oscar Olson, president of the Senate of Sweden, when she beat him at squares (connecting dots with lines to form the most boxes) twice in succession. Shirley's other set-side games included cribbage (which she learned at the age of five), checkers, parchesi and casino. She was at home with the studio wits, the fun-lovers and avoided anyone who seemed moody or preoccupied.

For this reason her least favorite director was Irving Cummings (*Curly Top, Poor Little Rich Girl*), a nervous, temperamental man who screamed if there was any noise on the set: "Give me a break—you see what I'm up against here, don't you? I've got a baby here, I'm working with a kid." Shirley was hurt and bewildered. Wasn't it okay to be a kid? She played scenes mechanically and didn't laugh much in the Cummings pictures, but when she changed directors again the legendary effervescent giggle came back.

On any set Shirley never quite seemed to be paying attention. When her mother, the director, or any other player coached her she would look down at her feet and roll her eyes around the room like any distracted youngster, and even bounce a ball or play jacks. But learning routines had started so early for her that she got them the first time while seeming to be doing something else. Her coaches seldom had to repeat instructions. In a single morning, less time than it took with adults, Bill Robinson taught her a soft shoe number, a waltz clog and three tap-dance routines. Shirley never looked at him once during this session but got all the numbers from listening to his feet.

Robinson, her idol and co-star in *The Little Colonel* and *The Littlest Rebel*, said she was the

In her *Stowaway* getup, Shirley peruses the latest in a long line of Temple publications.

An uncertain Shirley is vaccinated by her physician, Russell Sands, shortly after the shooting of *The Little Colonel*.

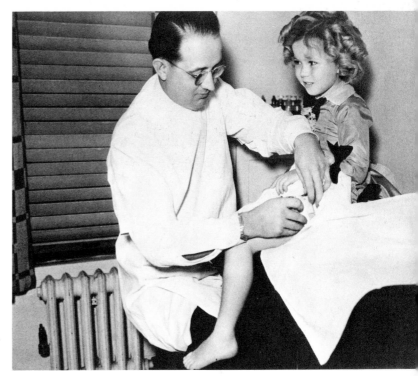

"Oh, my goodness" and the pursed lips were as much of a Temple trademark as the golden curls.

A doll and her carriage.

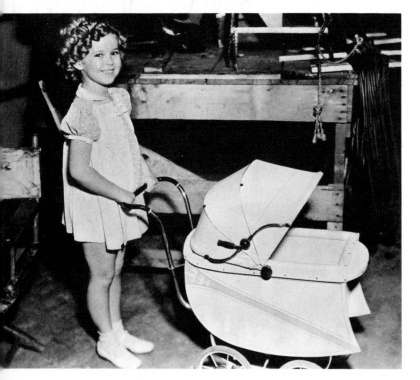

greatest tap dancer for her age then living, and he swore to make her the greatest in the world someday. She called him "Uncle Billy." He taught Shirley strenuous routines without letting her know it was work or allowing her to become tired.

"That was very copacetic, Shirley," he would say, "now we'll try it once more."

Or, "How'd you like to sit right down on that bench and watch your Uncle Bill do the routine? Then maybe he'll connect you with a nice Coca-Cola."

Or, "Bet you a nickel you can't do it again— who's gwine to be the judge?"

Jack Donahue, the choreographer of *Curly Top* and *Captain January*, was rehearsing a song called "You Take Two Steps and Truck on Down" with Shirley, and he asked Robinson, "What am I going to do then?"

"Why you truck on down," came the reply.

"Can she truck?" asked Donahue.

"Sure she can," replied Robinson.

When the scene was over Robinson got Shirley into a corner and asked, "Why didn't you tell Jack you could truck?"

"Don't be funny," she answered. "I'm not giving away any of our steps!"

During another Robinson–Temple routine some dancers from a neighboring production company came onto the set to watch them. Bill gave the signal to the pianist and said, "Come on, Shirley, let's do it." She shook her head no, uncharacteristically. Robinson took her aside and asked what was the matter. "If we do it now they'll steal it," she said. "We'll only do it when they're ready to shoot."

"I didn't have to look at Bill Robinson's feet when he was teaching me to dance," she remembered. "We had our mental symphony together, and he was a marvelous teacher, and I still remember some of his dances. He was the greatest."

Another of Shirley's idols was Will Rogers, with whom she never had the chance to make a movie. (He was killed in a plane crash in 1935.) But he taught her to ride and she often visited him at his ranch. She so admired the cowboy that after his death she would not let anyone sing or whistle his favorite song, "The Last Roundup," in her presence.

But throughout the next few years, Shirley's mother remained her most important coach. "Sparkle, Shirley, sparkle," she would call to her daughter at various times during filming. If Shirley had to cry in a scene, her mother would take her outside and give her a stern talking-to for several minutes. Back in front of the camera, Shirley cried without effort. "It's in the script," she said whenever she was asked if she minded crying on cue. Gertrude taught Shirley her parts by reading them aloud several times over after supper. Because this aural method of learning lines made it necessary to learn all the other parts in a script, Shirley often astonished her co-workers by correcting them when they muffed their dialogue. (She also infuriated at least one of them, Lionel Barrymore, when he forgot his lines. Shirley would say, "This is what you're supposed to say, Mr. Barrymore . . ." Actor Robert Young recalled "this made him furious—steam would come out of his ears." And Shirley remembered: "If I would say his lines, he would swear so much that I'd get sent home early. My teacher would say, 'You can't speak that way in front of a minor,' so I'd have a short day.")

"Mrs. Temple is much more Shirley's director than I am," said Irving Cummings. "She teaches her her lines, coaches her on how to say them, suggests Shirley's expressions, shows her how to stand and sit and walk and talk and run. There's really very little left for a director to do when Shirley arrives on the scene."

Shirley wasn't critical of her own performances, but what did interest her was seeing what scenes had been cut from the final prints of her movies; she was disappointed if one of her favorites was left out. Her only other serious complaint in her first two years at the Fox studios was that her bungalow didn't have a swing. The property department put one up on the tree next to her dressing room, but when a studio mogul saw her swinging high over Janet Gaynor's bungalow next door he ordered the swing removed. He didn't want the lot's biggest box-office draw to fall and hurt herself and the studio.

In March of 1935 Shirley was asked to put her foot- and handprints in the forecourt of Grauman's Chinese Theatre in Hollywood, and she wrote in her childish scrawl her message to the world: "Love to You All." In April her birthday party was postponed from the 23rd because she had the sniffles. "When Shirley sniffles, it costs us $5,000," said Buddy DeSylva, the producer of *The Little Colonel.*

Shirley Temple pictures had many distinguished co-stars but she really didn't need their support

By the new year 1936 Shirley was a self-assured star who was never seen in the same dress twice.

31

to sell her vehicles. That was a good thing, as most established actors were reluctant to work with a child anyway—since children invariably stole scenes. Lionel Barrymore had been adamant in refusing to appear with Shirley, but after *The Little Colonel* was completed the aging actor, living alone at the time and badly crippled with arthritis, said, "I feel like a happier man." He began to cry when Shirley asked him to sign her autograph book.

Gloria Stuart didn't want to appear with Shirley and was furious about the favoritism shown Shirley in camera angles on the remake of *Rebecca of Sunnybrook Farm*. Alice Faye *(Poor Little Rich Girl, Stowaway)* said to Gloria, "Why worry? Temple will steal the picture anyway." And Adolphe Menjou, her co-star in *Little Miss Marker*, said, "That Temple kid scares me. She knows all the tricks. She backs me out of the camera, blankets me, crabs my laughs. She's making a stooge of me. Well, she's an Ethel Barrymore at four."

In real life Shirley was given an allowance of $4.25 weekly, while the rest of her $1,000 salary was carefully invested by her father in gilt-edged securities, annuities and selected bonds, all picked with mid-Depression wariness. From the $4.25 Shirley put $1.50 in her toy bank and in a typical week in 1935 spent: on candy, 25 cents, fruit, 40 cents, soda pop, 15 cents, a box of paints, 75 cents, dog collar, 95 cents, and Sunday School collection, 25 cents.

In the fantasy world her movies were now making from $1 million to $1.5 million on their first releases alone—and this at a time when most of the audience—children—paid only 15 cents to get into the theatre. Temple routinely packed 2,000-seat houses in big cities for afternoon performances and did only slightly less well at night. Her pictures did even better on second and third runs. What made her box-office appeal even more extraordinary was the fact that her pictures were cheap to make, costing usually between $200,000–300,000. They had simple stories, few sets, mostly indoor, and small shooting companies. They were often brought in a week or ten days under their estimated shooting schedule.

At the end of 1935 Shirley "X"-ed, and her parents signed, a revised contract with 20th Century-Fox: $4,000 a week over all fifty-two weeks of the calendar year, a bonus of more than $20,000 per picture plus $500 a week for Gertrude. Under product tie-in deals with ten firms for Shirley

Temple dolls, and underwear, coats, hats, shoes, books, hair ribbons, soap, dresses, toys, cereal bowls and milk pitchers, she recived another $1,000 a week (and her mother an additional $100 a week).

Besides being the most important screen actress, Shirley Temple quickly became the most important singer on screen. By introducing a song in a movie she automatically made it a hit, and top song writers of the day such as Harry Warren, Irving Caesar, Paul Francis Webster, Richard Whiting and Mack Gordon turned out material for Shirley. Sheet music for her "Polly Wolly Doodle" and "On The Good Ship Lollipop" ran over 400,000 copies each, topping the sales of any song introduced in the same period by Bing Crosby, Nelson Eddy, Alice Faye or any other movie singer. Her 1935 Shirley Temple Christmas songbook sold 250,000 copies. And her popularity was worldwide as well. In Japan, where she was also the top box-office star, a thirty-six-page book of pictures of Shirley, with no text in any language, sold over 1,200,000 copies.

The lives of George and Gertrude Temple were drastically altered by their daughter's accession to the top ranks of movie stars. At the beginning of 1934 George was just a bank teller at the California Bank branch at 16th and Vermont in Los Angeles. He was quickly promoted to branch manager after his bank showed a marked increase in children's savings accounts. Just before Shirley's eighth birthday, in April of 1936, George was promoted to manager of the larger branch of the California Bank at Hollywood and Cahuenga Boulevards in Hollywood. He moved his family from their modest six-room frame house in Santa Monica to a larger house in Brentwood canyon, banked on a hillside, and protected on two sides by canyon walls to give the dimpled star privacy from the hordes of enthusiastic fans whose curiosity knew no hours.

The old LaSalle was traded in for a long black Cadillac, and now Shirley was always accompanied on the lot and in public by her chauffeur-bodyguard, John Griffith. Griffith, six-foot-two and two hundred pounds, had been given the job by Darryl Zanuck, whom he had saved from drowning when both were boys in Nebraska. Zanuck had arrived at Fox in 1935 just in time to produce *The Littlest Rebel*, when Shirley's legs started to grow long. Zanuck told his Fox underlings to keep her doll-like dresses short and to have her co-

J. Edgar Hoover made Shirley a G-woman and earned a kiss, 1936.

A total tomboy if not a natural athlete, she tried every sport and game at least once.

Fan mags weren't a staple in Shirley's life, but she sure was in theirs.

One of Shirley's most successful merchandising efforts was this hat, which little girls and their mothers snapped up by the tens of thousands, especially at Easter.

She was born in the seacoast city of Santa Monica, and at fifty she liked to fish as much as she had at five.

stars lifts her up a lot to preserve the illusion of her little-girl lightness.

Shirley had succeeded in hospitalizing "Griff" for exhaustion for two days in Palm Springs, despite his size and strength. He had chased her for miles in the resort, burdened with his hardware and heavy clothes in the hot sun, while she, having just learned to ride a bicycle, got away from him and escaped down a dusty street. Griff's wife later became Mrs. Temple's personal maid.

George, Gertrude and Shirley attempted to take a normal family vacation in the summer of 1935 and sailed off to Hawaii for twelve weeks. But her adoring fans saw them off and greeted their return home. In Honolulu, in near-riot conditions Shirley was made a member of the Safety Patrol of the Hawaiian resort and presented by the Japanese colony in the territory with what they termed "the finest and most elaborate bridal doll ever to reach Hawaii; its value is beyond dollars and cents." It was twice as tall as Shirley.

Neither of Shirley's brothers, Jack or George, Jr. (Sonny), had a spark of interest or ambition in show business, although Jack was given a job for a few months in the Fox publicity department, with no qualifications other than being Shirley's brother. He begged to be allowed to go to Stanford instead, and no one refused him, although at college his fellow students elected him manager of the Stanford Dramatic Club, hoping that something of his little sister had rubbed off on him.

It was Gertrude whose life was truly changed, however. She kept insisting that "if the day ever comes when I feel that Shirley is becoming self-conscious or too aware of her screen importance I shall cancel her contract immediately and let her grow up to a normal girlhood, far from Hollywood and its studios." But in the meantime, not only did Gertrude have to take care of the child who was suddenly the most beloved and photographed human being in the world, she also felt compelled to tell how she did it in a flood of articles for women's magazines. "I do not let Shirley get the idea that she is too important in our scheme of existence," she wrote. "At home she feels everything revolves around her father."

Shirley was disciplined when necessary and Gertrude even felt that it would be a good idea for her daughter to get a public spanking in a film, as an example to children and their parents, but the studio wouldn't hear of it. Personal appear-

34

ances by Shirley, which could have earned her a lot of additional money, were vetoed by George and Gertrude because the public's adulation would be direct and possibly harmful. "The mother of a famous star has a difficult road to travel," concluded Gertrude Temple. "No mother can know how difficult until she has a small celebrity in her own home."

When she was ten years old, Shirley Temple decided to be a Republican, for what she admitted was a "facetious" reason. (But she nonetheless stuck with the G.O.P. throughout her life.) On a promotional trip back East she stopped in Boston, where Mayor Curley still held sway. Shirley visited him at City Hall. "When we came out," she recalled, "there were lots of fans around his car and everyone was getting fingerprints on his black limousine, and it made him annoyed. I was leaning out of the car waving goodbye, and Mayor Curley was so upset about all those fans getting fingerprints on his car that when he got in he slammed the door on my four fingers. They're still slightly bent. I found out that Mayor Curley was a Democrat and thought that was a good reason to pick out the other party, so I started early."

Out in public in the period 1936–1940, Mayor Curley notwithstanding, Shirley was lionized and accorded just about every formal accolade short of an honorary university degree. The week of her eighth birthday in 1936 (which the innocent world thought was only her seventh) she became the youngest person ever to appear on the cover of Time, and the story inside displayed her forged birth certificate. Also the youngest person ever to be listed in Who's Who, Shirley's capsule biography was nineteen lines long, eight longer than Greta Garbo's, the next most prominent from the show business world.

Shirley was also an honorary Kentucky Colonel, a Captain of the Texas Rangers, a member of the staff of the Governor of Idaho, mascot of the Chilean Navy and president of the 400,000-member Chum's Club of Scotland—and of the Kiddies Club of England (whose 165,000 members pledged to imitate her character, conduct and manners). She received 3,500 fan letters a week, 1,100 of them from people over the age of fifty. On New Year's Day 1939, Shirley was Grand Marshal of the Rose Bowl Parade in Pasadena ("the coldest day of my life," she recalled. "We had to get on the floats at four o'clock in the morning").

The President of the United States, Franklin D. Roosevelt, was "her willing slave all afternoon" when Shirley visited him in Washington, D.C., in 1937. (They talked about—among other things—fishing and the rigors of travel.) Mrs. Eleanor Roosevelt dropped by the set of Little Miss Broadway, intending to stay for about fifteen minutes and watch one of Shirley's dance numbers with George Murphy. "We immediately fell twenty minutes behind schedule," Senator Murphy recalled. "Because as soon as Shirley met somebody she touched them; nobody told her to do it or how to do it, she just did it."

"Mrs. Roosevelt stayed for two hours," Shirley remembered, "and then we had lunch together in my bungalow. She invited me to visit her at Hyde Park, New York, where she personally did a barbecue for me. I asked her 'What do you do?' and she told me of her interest in the people of the world and how she was trying to improve the lot of people in my country and make suggestions to the League of Nations. She made quite an impression on me."

Apart from the 100,000 feet of film in which she appeared every year, Shirley Temple was the most photogaphed human being in the world in the mid-1930s, not excluding President Roosevelt or the Prince of Wales. She was the only American besides Babe Ruth to be universally adored in Japan. And the Greeks had a special word of endearment for her. Since the world's great visited her at the studio, Shirley acquired one of the world's great autograph collections.

The only killjoy on the scene seemed to be Graham Greene, then a film critic, who wrote in a British magazine (after a visit to Hollywood during which he spent long hours on the set at 20th Century-Fox) that Shirley was a thirty-year-old midget, married and with a seven-year-old child of her own. On Shirley's behalf 20th Century-Fox and Gertrude and George sued and won. Greene's magazine went out of business, and the settlement went into a trust in a London bank until Shirley turned twenty-one and gave it to charity, for the building of a youth center in England.

At home at playtime Shirley's activities somewhat belied her screen image. For one thing, she was fonder of guns than of dolls. "I had a Roy Rogers flare gun, cap pistols, everything," she said. She told a visitor who turned out to be the president of a gun factory of her interest, and he sent her an air rifle. "But I only got a glimpse of

Whether swabby . . .

. . . or admiral, Shirley was a military girl.

She was also a ballerina . . .

. . . a ragamuffin . . .

36

... aviatrix ...

... a bus driver ...

... and cowgirl.

37

it. I was a tomboy back in Santa Monica. We had four acres of wild forest around us. I had a horse and a neighborhood gang, mostly boys. I was a bluejeans and T-shirt kind of little girl. I climbed trees, took archery and swam a lot. I wanted to join the FBI and be the first woman G-man; in fact, J. Edgar Hoover made me one." She in turn organized the Shirley Temple Police Force and inducted Hoover, Mrs. Roosevelt and all cast and crew members on all her pictures. There were fines for not wearing the badges and not keeping them brightly shined (the money later built boys' and girls' clubs in Santa Monica).

Shirley also went through a period, when she was seven, of wanting to be a pie-seller. "My parents were building a new house," she said, "and I would take pie tins and fill them with cement to sell to the tourists who would come by the house. Of course they wanted a pie that had been made by Shirley Temple, but I thought they really wanted them. I believed in what I was selling. There was no false advertising at all, no handprint in them or anything. They were just plain old cement pies. That job lasted a couple of days until my mother got wind of it. I made five cents a pie."

The Shirley Temple pictures of the 1936–39 period—all of them star vehicles specifically created or adapted for her—continued to set box-office records. And while she was still telling corny jokes ("There were three holes in the ground . . . well, well, well!"), she was supremely aware of her position on the 20th Century-Fox lot. Some journalists were interviewing Gertrude Temple and other movie mothers and guardians one day when Shirley sauntered over to say: "Why don't you talk to me? I'm the star."

Even as she grew taller, and lost her curls to a center part and two pony tails, Darryl Zanuck, a producer at 20th Century-Fox, was forced to agree with her assessments. In general, he believed that pictures were more important than stars, but he thought, "Shirley Temple is endless. There's no one in the world to compare with that child. I've made eight pictures with her, and each time I'm knocked dead. It's just beyond the case of being a freak. This child has rhythm. I always thought when we dropped the curls—this is the end. This mint, this gold mine had gone dry. But now she's good for years." (His optimism aside, Zanuck increased the budgets on her films and gave her stronger supporting casts.)

While she was still child enough to be excited because there was a flood at 20th Century-Fox during the filming of Little Miss Broadway "and nobody was gonna be allowed to leave the studio," Shirley was "nearly adult and perfectly natural in her reactions," recalled her co-star (and later U.S. senator) George Murphy. "Her emotions were real and the director never seemed to have problems with her." When she was deciding whether or not to run for Congress in 1967, she visited Murphy in Los Angeles to ask his advice. "Her potential campaign was just as well-organized as she had been in pictures," he said. "And I told her that her good common sense would be an asset in Congress."

Gertrude Temple remained, in director Allan Dwan's view, the real creative genius. "Shirley was the product of her mother," he said. "Shirley was the instrument on which her mother played. I don't know why the mother was like that—but I'd seen it before with Mary Pickford and her domineering mother. As a director, whenever I wanted anything from Shirley, I looked at the mother."

Dwan served for his three pictures with Shirley (Heidi, Rebecca of Sunnybrook Farm, Young People) as Captain of the Shirley Temple Police Force; Shirley of course was Chief. For years he kept a supply of badges and whenever he was stopped for speeding would whip one out. Though it was a fake and Shirley was passe, the gift of one to a policeman usually prevented a ticket. "She'd had her peak and was sliding fast when I started working with her in 1938," Dwan recalled. "But it was such a pleasure working with her—I never saw her anger or annoy anyone—that it was a shame to take the money. It was sad that the spark lasted only to a certain age. But if Shirley Temple was only a moment in movie history, it was a great moment."

In 1940, after two flops in a row, The Blue Bird and Young People (which, fittingly, was about a little girl who grows up and tries to become just like other girls) George and Gertrude Temple bought up the remainder of Shirley's contract from 20th Century-Fox and sent her off to real school. Shirley had stopped believing in Santa Claus when one in a department store asked for her autograph and had worn her first long dress at her eleventh birthday party. She took the decision stoically.

Westlake School for Girls in Los Angeles was

These cowgirls never got the blues.

The little queen of 20th Century-Fox holds a press conference.

The doll and her doll, 1935.

To the delight of her fans in the Hawaiian Islands, Shirley, her father and mother took a vacation there in 1936, and it became the first of many.

39

Every time she went to Hawaii she got a big deal "aloha."

She quickly picked up the hula in Honolulu.

Only Disney characters like the Seven Dwarfs seriously rivalled Shirley's popularity among tots in the 1930s. Gertrude and George Temple beam in the background.

Her whole grade school education was conducted by Frances Klampt (Klammie) at the studio.

No holiday went by without Shirley's talking turkey (or pumpkins, Santa Claus, Baby New Year, hearts, shamrocks etc.).

The world's princess waves her wand to welcome the New Year.

Shirley tests the sharpness of Sonia Henie's skates.

In the mid-1930s kids ate their spinach and breakfasts because this girl said they should.

an exclusive, expensive country day school, as close to an Eastern "prep" school as anything in California when Shirley enrolled there in 1940 at age twelve. Her parents put her there, she said, "so that I would know what competition was. I spent the first year in that school looking at all the other girls' hairstyles, and they told me all the latest jokes. I grew up rapidly once I got into that school. At the studio I hadn't had much to do with other children because we were working and they were with their tutors also."

Shirley was not retiring from movies, Gertrude carefully explained, but until she was through with school her time at work would be limited and the properties carefully chosen. No new contracts were signed but rumors were plentiful. Mrs. Temple turned down three Broadway musicals, including an *Uncle Tom's Cabin* in swingtime and Cole Porter's *Dubarry Was a Lady,* starring Ethel Merman, but was open to a radio deal.

Along with other girls at school, Shirley listened to President Roosevelt's defense message in the spring of 1940, made notes and talked about it with her family when she got home. But war talk in general upset her since brothers Jack, aged twenty-five, a graduate student at Stanford, and George, twenty-one, at home in Brentwood, were very vulnerable to the draft. Her preferred radio fare consisted of serials like "Little Orphan Annie" and "Superman" from 5:30-6:30 P.M. when the four Temples sat down to dinner. And even on the road activity ceased when "The Lone Ranger" hit the airwaves.

Shirley spent her summer vacation between seventh and eighth grades at Westlake taking swimming lessons, pecking away at a typewriter with no special writing to do, and playing with her girlfriends Mary Lou Islieb and Harold Lloyd's daughters Peggy and Gloria. Sometimes she made as many as three daily trips to the main gate in front of the Temple compound to give out autographs and wave to the tour buses. She sidewalk-superintended the building of her elaborate playhouse, whose architecture was English lodge house. Its main feature was a small theatre with a proscenium stage and velvet curtains at one end and seats for eighty-five people. The auditorium could be converted for dancing. There were also special rooms for her doll collection, unanswered fan mail, and games. A regulation duckpin bowling alley was in the basement. On her three trips to Honolulu, Shirley had delightedly discovered slot machines, and one was included there too.

She had given up riding six months before when two girlfriends were killed in accidents with horses, and the Temples sold her two ponies and her horse, which had been stabled in the backyard. Twentieth Century-Fox's chairman Nicholas Schenk had imported a Shetland pony from the Shetland Islands as a present for her, and it remained as an unridden pet, along with three small dogs. The Temples kept a cook and maid, and a chauffeur to drive Shirley to work or school in a Pontiac station wagon. Her only professional appearance in several months was on a Red Cross coast-to-coast radio broadcast in which Shirley did a melodramatic skit with Paul Muni.

However, old habits die hard, and by late 1941, Shirley Temple was back at work. She did four shows for Lux soap at $5,000 per show and a four-part "Shirley Temple Time" for Elgin at the same salary. On the first of the Elgin shows the announcer introduced Shirley as "America's Little Sweetheart," and it seemed for a while that the buildup was on to place her on Mary Pickford's long unoccupied throne. (Pickford and Temple had recently been photographed together for *Life* as a couple of has-beens.) During the dress rehearsal Shirley had induced a few sentimental tears from the audience, but dressed in blue velveteen, squinching her nose, smiling sweetly and throwing off virginal vibrations as a five-foot, 101-pound thirteen-year-old, her actual on-the-air reading of lines left the audience dry-eyed.

Mama Temple, as before, was in back-up attendance at the broadcast and George Sr. announced that there were "half a dozen more good offers." Shirley herself said about live radio: "It's adorable. I get a big thrill out of it, and I want to do as much radio work as I can. I like it because you have to do it right the first time. In pictures, if it's wrong, you can do it over."

Less than a year after she quit movies Louis B. Mayer at MGM signed Shirley for her comeback at a salary of $50,000 per picture or $2,500 a week, humiliating when stacked against her last salary for 20th Century-Fox, $300,000 or $9,000. No longer blonde or chubby, Shirley posed for publicity stills with MGM's top stars Mickey Rooney and Judy Garland with an announcement that the three juveniles would appear together in *Babes in Arms*, and in the Andy Hardy series. But her actual comeback was *Kathleen*, the making of

Horsing around in Brentwood, 1937.

Her own line of bathing suits was just a small part of the merchandising of Shirley Temple.

43

For her ninth birthday she got a bike and a sudden mature child look that had studio chieftains worrying about how long the goldmine could last.

Irving Berlin (left) and his daughter Mary Ellin visited Shirley and director Allan Dwan on the *Heidi* set.

Not many little girls get to go sailing in their own swimming pools between pictures.

Even as a child, Shirley lent her name and time to worthy causes.

44

which, in the summer and fall of 1941, Shirley described as "a wonderful vacation—no school or anything, just fun, like it used to be." The MGM contract was cancelled by mutual consent, after the failure of *Kathleen*. Her second comeback film was no better. *Miss Annie Rooney* was an outdated, low-budget rehash released through United Artists. She retired again, for almost two years.

Shirley was at Westlake enough of the time to sustain a B average, and there she threw herself into the role of a snappy wartime teenager of her day. She participated in freshman hazing—wearing a sunbonnet and shining seniors' shoes with a toothbrush for a week—and went to dances in long dresses with military academy boys. She wore an ankle bracelet and too much lipstick—except when her mother lay "in wait for me, brandishing a Kleenex," which was most of the time. She also wore a standard navy blue Westlake uniform except that she had wide Adrian-style shoulders added. "Got to have some glamour," she explained.

Still, the Temples and Shirley were serious about a movie comeback, and she took voice lessons and studied with drama coach Robert Graham Paris. Paris escorted her one night in 1943 to the Hollywood Canteen, the USO's star-studded haven for servicemen on leave in the Los Angeles area. Mrs. John Ford was in charge

45

EXECUTIVE DEPARTMENT
Office of the Mayor
ATLANTIC CITY, N.J.

APRIL 4, 1938.

MISS SHIRLEY TEMPLE,
HOLLYWOOD, CALIF.
DEAR SHIRLEY -

ON BEHALF OF ALL OF OUR CITIZENS I AM
EXTENDING A MOST SINCERE INVITATION TO YOU
TO COME TO ATLANTIC CITY, AS OUR GUEST, FOR
CHILDREN'S WEEK, JUNE 24 TO JULY 1.

THE AFFAIR IS AN ANNUAL EVENT DURING
WHICH THE RESORT PROVIDES A SPECIAL PROGRAM
FOR ITS YOUNGER GUESTS FROM ALL SECTIONS OF
THE WORLD. EVERY DAY OFFERS SOMETHING NEW
IN THE WAY OF ENTERTAINMENT AND WE ARE SURE
YOU WOULD HAVE A MOST ENJOYABLE VISIT.

WE HAVE BEEN GIVEN TO UNDERSTAND THAT
YOU WILL BE IN THE EAST AT THAT TIME AND WE
HOPE THAT YOU WILL FIND IT POSSIBLE TO ACCEPT
THIS INVITATION TO COME TO ATLANTIC CITY.
SINCERELY,

C.D.White

MAYOR

ATLANTIC CITY

Who could refuse an invitation that imposing? Not Shirley.

At age ten Shirley Temple wasn't too old for dolls—at least not in a Studio Publicity Shot for Christmas 1938.

Knitting a sweater on the set of *The Blue Bird*.

Jackie Oakie was a captive subject for Shirley's Brownie.

Easter of 1939 had Shirley got up as a choir girl and plugging *Susannah of the Mounties*.

and Bette Davis had suggested Shirley to sell kisses. In spite of all the concern for her safety, which included being ushered in through the kitchen, fifteen-year-old Shirley stayed to jitterbug the night away.

"Shirley was never allowed to know that she was anything special," Paris recalled, "even in her 'adult' movie years. She was still asked to do chores like making beds and not to behave like a star; Jane Withers, on the other hand, was encouraged to run around with a Hollywood crowd. The Temples were the most normal of families in a town full of abnormal families. Shirley didn't really become a woman during those years. She didn't become a woman until she became a politician."

David O. Selznick, who already had Ingrid Bergman, Joan Fontaine, Jennifer Jones and Joseph Cotten under contract, signed Shirley Temple to a seven-year personal contract in 1944 and announced as her first vehicle *Since You Went Away*, his self-written tribute to the American family in wartime. Selznick billed Shirley only fourth—after Claudette Colbert, Jones and Cotten —and was anxious to have the film regarded as another major star-studded Selznick epic (his first since *Gone with the Wind*) and not as a vehicle for Temple's comeback. But in spite of his best efforts to the contrary, *Since You Went Away* was in large part just that.

Selznick gave Shirley a sweet sixteen birthday party on the set of *Since You Went Away*, which was still standing during filming of *I'll Be Seeing You* with Ginger Rogers and Cotten, thus continuing a tradition that began when she was five but hadn't been observed for three years. Because of the war the party was kept deliberately simple, and lasted exactly one hour. Its total cost was $46.11: cake, $24; five gallons of vanilla ice cream, $17.50; and three boxes of candy, $4.61. Members of the cast and crew gave Shirley roses and Selznick gave her a silver bracelet with a heart attached.

All other gifts were gags. Ginger Rogers gave Shirley a John Fredericks hat made of chicken feathers, while Cotten presented her with a box of paper balls that exploded and jumped when the lid was opened. Mary Lou Islieb, who was still Shirley's stand-in, gave her a dribbling water glass, Jennifer Jones a make-up book and Tom Tully a rubber hot dog (the real kind being Shirley's favorite food). Dare Harris, who was seventeen

At her 'eleventh" birthday in 1940 Shirley serves up cake for some other kids on the lot.

A junior shutterbug on the set of *Young People* in 1940, Shirley was already at the awkward-looking twelve-year-old stage, and past her box-office prime.

49

MGM's Louis B. Mayer and Shirley made a deal for her "comeback" at thirteen, but after one picture (*Kathleen*) the contract was cancelled by mutual consent.

Since she went away voluntarily, Shirley had to mean it when she marched back to work in *Kathleen* during junior high school.

In her teens Shirley still liked to play games during idle moments on the set.

50

and one of Shirley's dates, gave her a fake news-paper front page with the headline: "Shirley Temple Will Be 65 In 1993."

Mrs. Temple gave her daughter just what she needed, another doll (an antique French one) and "Joy" perfume, Shirley's favorite. Mr. Temple came up with more "Joy," a gold pin and an Eversharp fountain pen. Brother Jack sent flowers and classical record albums. Shirley's dress for the occasion was a gray chiffon over pink with a bodice of cut embroidery, from a new film then in the making.

Despite her advanced years (and having achieved her full adult height of five-feet-two), Shirley was still required to have three hours of school on the set and one hour of recreation (walking, reading, talking with friends) before 4 P.M. Lunch had to be at 12:30 and she had to be off the set by 6 P.M. Shirley had a much freer choice in her clothing and social life. She some-times went on dates without chaperons and was allowed to use the Temple car and chauffeur. Dare Harris, who was in *I'll Be Seeing You* (having been discovered by a Selznick talent scout in a bowling alley), was not Shirley's favorite date—he wasn't in uniform, after all. But he was ardent in his pursuit, once following the Temples to Palm Springs and camping out in the desert because there were no available hotel rooms.

The two wartime Temple–Selznick films were released in rapid succession and Selznick was excited by the reaction to Shirley Temple. In one of the producer's famous memos, he wrote at the end of 1944: "Shirley is exceedingly hot at the moment. We can't commence to fill demands for interviews and other press material on her from newspapers and magazines; and this is, of course, an indication of the interest of the public. At the preview of *I'll Be Seeing You* . . . Shirley's name was received with the biggest applause of all three (stars) despite the fact that the Gallup poll shows that Cotten is the great new romantic rage, and that Ginger is one of the top stars in the business.

"Shirley's publicity in the New York press, both in connection with this appearance and in con-nection with her prior trip East to sell bonds, re-ceived more publicity—including, astonishingly, big front-page breaks in the middle of a war—than I think has been accorded the visit of any motion-picture star to New York in many, many years . . . . Her fan mail is greater than that of any other star on our list—actually exceeding by a

Only after she turned thirteen did Shirley Temple herself become clothes-conscious; she took up sewing during *Kathleen* and designed some of her clothes on this small mannequin.

51

Choreographer Nick Castle (*second from left*) teaches Olsen, Johnson and Temple some steps for *Hellzapoppin*, but the picture went into production without her.

In 1943, when she was fifteen, and Mary Pickford was fifty, *Life* called them "has-beens." *Credit: Fred Parrish for LIFE*

wide margin that of Ingrid Bergman, Jennifer Jones and Joan Fontaine, who are the next three in that order . . . ."

For all that, the producer soon became preoccupied with Jennifer Jones, who was divorcing Robert Walker and would later marry Selznick, and he lost interest in developing the career of a second ingenue. While he kept Shirley under contract, the rest of her films would be on loanout to other studios.

When she turned seventeen in 1945, Shirley had been a movie star for eleven years; her every move had been chronicled for millions of adoring fans, even during the Westlake School years and her recent return to films in supporting roles. Still, she yearned for a more normal American lifestyle, and she tried very hard to attain it. Much too hard, it turned out. "I made a lot of decisions when I was seventeen," she recalled. "One of them was to get married, and I did. I wanted marriage more than a career, because you can get awfully lonely with your scrapbooks when you find yourself at the end of your career. What it's really all about is marriage and family as far as I'm concerned."

Graduation from Westlake School for Girls

Even as a teenager Shirley daily greeted fans at the fence surrounding her parents' Brentwood home.

came first, three months before her wedding in September. "It was a beautiful June morning," she remembered, "and we all wore long white dresses down to the ground and carried bouquets of red roses, all identical. The dresses were alike so no one would look different from anyone else; we all bought them at the same place. V-J Day was in August of 1945, so the war was almost at an end, and we were looking forward to all of our friends—sometimes very close friends—coming back from military service.

"And we were looking forward to the end of gas rationing and butter rationing and meatless Tuesdays and all the things that were part of the war years. Gas rationing was the hardest part for us teenagers. We liked to go around in cars, and we'd have to plan very carefully how far we could go on half a tank of gas, or a quarter of a tank. Very often we'd have to turn off the motor and coast down hills and carefully start again at the bottom. That was the biggest hazard in dating, besides getting home on time," she said.

One of the most normal things about Shirley in her teens during World War II was that she was boy-crazy. Ever since her first little-girl crushes on her male co-stars, Shirley had reserved her most special affection for the men in her life

(something that would later stand her in exceptionally good stead in the mostly male world of international diplomacy). She dated frequently, co-star Guy Madison and songwriter Nacio Herb Brown, among others, and retained her greatest fondness for men in uniform. And the one returning serviceman most likely to keep her out late was John Agar.

Agar, a member of a Chicago meat packing family, was a sergeant in the Army Air Force and a physical training instructor at California's March Field. He was handsome, blond, six feet two, and had first met Shirley in 1943 at a tea given by ZaSu Pitts, the Temples' next-door neighbor in Brentwood. In the early spring of 1945, even before Shirley's seventeenth birthday, "Jack" Agar and Shirley Temple decided to get married. He presented her with a dazzling two-and-a-half-carat square-cut diamond, which she wore under a glove on her left hand at an April Sunday luncheon in a Beverly Hills restaurant for the forty-three members of the senior class at Westlake.

She unthinkingly took off the glove, and when her schoolmates questioned her about the diamond, Shirley fled, flustered, to the ladies' room. All forty-three girls followed her, giggling, and

53

Ching-Ching, a Pekinese, played with Shirley in *Stowaway* but had long since retired from films by 1943.

Mary Lou Isleib, Shirley's best friend and long-time stand-in, and Shirley share a milkshake at the Selznick studio commissary between scenes of *Since You Went Away*.

soon the whole restaurant knew what was going on. Later that afternoon at her parents' home Shirley dimpled a lot, and told the hastily summoned reporters that what she liked most about Jack was his "sincerity." The senior Temples, who had not wanted even to announce the engagement at least until Shirley had graduated from high school, nervously added: "Shirley and John have promised not to get married for two years, possibly three."

Shirley's birthday was two weeks after the engagement announcement. She spent a quiet day with John and a quiet evening with him and some friends who shared her cake. The next afternoon, however, was turned over to a promotional birthday party fostered by the United Nations Clothing Collection. On the purported grounds that Shirley was a big girl now and interested in international problems, the organization talked Mrs. Temple into parting with many of Shirley's little-girl dresses, including a few from the movies, and most with her name tags still in them. Some of the dresses Gertrude "just couldn't bear to part with. After all," she explained, "there might be a little girl in the family sometime and wouldn't she like to wear some of the things that her mother once wore in pictures?"

Still, some seventy-five garments were piled on a big chair in the Brentwood library and the press was invited in. The press release for the event said that Shirley had decided her first "adult" good deed would be to help the thirty million children in war-devastated countries. "It makes me happy to have a part in rebuilding the lives of girls my age or younger," she said. "Shirley Temple is vitally interested in the future peace of the world and believes that through the United National Clothing Collection every American has the privilege of helping to fashion this peace," said the handout. There was another seventeen-candle cake, and almost an hour of posing with clothing drive posters, her dimples and diamond flashing, before John—as previously scheduled—called her on the telephone.

The promise to her parents notwithstanding, Shirley Jane Temple became Mrs. John G. Agar at 8:59 P.M. on the evening of September 19, 1945. Six hundred guests, including California Governor Earl Warren (whose arrival delayed the 8:30 starting time) and David O. Selznick, witnessed the twelve-minute double-ring Episcopal ceremony at the Wilshire Methodist Church. Except for Miss

The once and future movie princess at the piano in her Brentwood living room and very much in the shadow of the little girl, 1943.

Like most 1940s teenagers Shirley loved convertible coupes.

In 1944, Shirley had her first date at New York's fabled Stork Club, and she danced the night away with Lieutenant Barney Straus of the Army Air Corps.

Pitts, who came solely in her capacity as next-door neighbor and friend, there were no movie stars in attendance, and George and Gertrude tried to keep the proceedings—within limits—dignified. Family and school friends, important members of the press and cameramen and crew from Shirley's early pictures, in evening clothes and furs, predominated.

They arched on tiptoe and craned their necks to see little Shirley, dressed in white satin and preceded by sixteen attendants, march down the aisle on George Sr.'s arm, playing this latest role with her usual poise, grace and dignity. Her dress had a fitted bodice, short sleeves and a "Little Infanta" skirt; the low round neck was edged by a looped cord of satin closely studded with seed pearls, with seed pearls also spattered over the bodice. The headdress holding her veils was a crown of corded satin wired in small loops. Her train was full and long, and the wrist-length satin gloves were scalloped and embroidered with seed pearls. She carried a bouquet of bovardia and white orchids; and a lace handkerchief for something borrowed, a small garter for something blue, a small cross worn inside her dress for something old, and Jack's wedding ring for something new. For good luck she put a penny in her shoe.

Turning sweet sixteen on the Selznick lot with a scaled-down party because of the War.

During the war years Shirley spent much of her free time in her dressing room writing letters to servicemen.

The clothes and the pose on the telephone were proto-typical teen-types of the 1940s . . .

While the soundstage picnic-for-one was a total fraud.

Shirley reached a second peak of movie popularity at sixteen, but it was straight downhill thereafter.

Jack Temple's wife was matron of honor and she and the seven bridesmaids (who included Phoebe Hearst and Mary Lou Islieb, Shirley's stand-in and best friend) wore dresses and cartwheel hats of "Temple Blue," a new color named by designer Louella Brantingham. The altar of the church was banked with pink and red roses and several tall candelabra. The center aisle was ribboned off in blue and groupings of green ferns were sporadically placed around the church. During the actual wedding vows, Shirley kept looking up at John, but displayed no other emotion. Both bride and groom stayed calm.

Several thousand fans, who had begun gathering at noon, screamed outside the church, pushed against the ring of military and local police who were trying to keep them roped off, and turned the relatively quiet affair into a Hollywood wedding, reminiscent of the Vilma Banky–Rod La-Rocque nuptials in 1927. The corner stoplight was top-heavy with little boys who had shinnied up it to achieve a better vantage point. For blocks in all directions cars were parked bumper to bumper. When Shirley and John tried to leave the church and pose on the steps for photographers the crowd surged forth into the church for fifteen minutes until the police could again rope them off. In the meantime Shirley refused one woman an autograph, saying she couldn't write with her gloves on.

In front of the Temple home in Brentwood flagstone flooring was especially laid down for the reception. A white three-tiered cake was on display, roped off under a canopy. Under a larger canopy in the center of the lawn small tables were grouped for eating and drinking, and the wedding party greeted well-wishers under still a third tent on the sidelines. A gypsy orchestra wandered through the crowd of 600. David Selznick was very visible, usually among the nubile bridesmaids. Once the actual ceremony was over, the wedding became a David O. Selznick production in the grand manner. Photographers were issued passes (one to a magazine or agency) by his publicity office to get past police lines and were promised and had delivered to them the bridal party for fifteen minutes at the church and thirty minutes at home before the reception, for pictures.

While John and Shirley received, their guests consumed twenty cases of Cresta Blanca champagne and countless platters of hors d'oeuvres.

58

Andre De Dienes, the photographer who discovered Marilyn Monroe, tried to make Shirley sexy too, but the public wouldn't have it. *Credit: Andre De Dienes*

Shirley read parts in radio plays while waiting for the right film.

Shirley got a public service award from Rudy Vallee on network radio.

What the well-dressed teen was wearing on Easter Sunday.

It's too late for Dore Schary to worry about Shirley Temple's growing up.

Between comeback films, Shirley did a lot of live radio, here with Fred Allen.

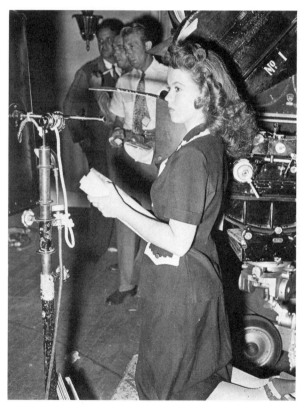

Always available to watch Joseph Cotten work, Shirley interrupts her script study during *I'll Be Seeing You*.

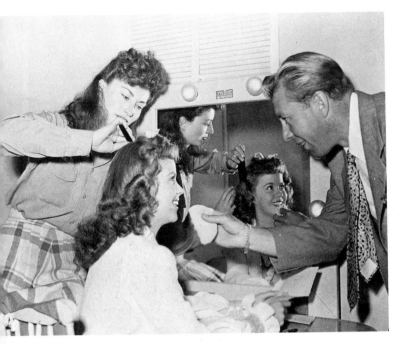

Makeup and hair are usually more important to a teen than to a tot.

After Shirley went to work for David Selznick, Gertrude Temple was replaced as hairdresser.

They visited Shirley's palatial former playhouse on the property, now containing nine long banquet tables full of wedding presents. The presents ranged from a Capehart radio console from Selznick and sheer table linen from the Darryl Zanucks to can openers, a frying pan, three cookbooks, and two dozen roses from the San Jose Fire Department. Mrs. Agar gave the newlyweds flat silver in a King Richard pattern and the Temples presented the bride and groom with a silver service set.

After the receiving line, Shirley and John, followed by their wedding party, wandered over to the playhouse. Shirley smoked as she walked down the path, and drank champagne openly. Near midnight she and John cut the wedding cake for a phalanx of photographers. Before going upstairs to change she threw her bouquet to the bridesmaids. Half an hour later she reappeared wearing a dove-gray wool suit with powder blue trim and beret, and the couple ran to the Temple driveway under a shower of rice to a new-looking station wagon that would take them on their honeymoon of seven days—all that was left of John's furlough.

The Agars' wedding night was spent at the Town House in Los Angeles, and the rest of their honeymoon in Santa Barbara, ninety miles northwest. When they arrived at the Town House at 1:15 A.M. on the 20th a newly-wed army major and his bride who had arrived a few hours before had mistakenly been given the Temple–Agar suite. Embarrassed night clerks obtained another suite, without flowers. "Anyway, I got the right husband," Shirley giggled.

Or so it seemed for a while. After John returned to his base, Shirley moved in with George and Gertrude and supervised the refurbishing of her playhouse on the four-acre estate into a honeymoon cottage. "We'll put up a fence," Shirley said. "You'd better," said her mother, "we don't want your dogs and kids running over here." Shirley enrolled in a cooking school. "At least I'd better know how to cook for John," she said. "I want to fix his first supper after we remodel our house. I'll serve him Spam and beans; he's got to feel at home."

Apart from her marriage, Shirley looked and behaved pretty much as any other seventeen-year-old living at home with her parents. She had a dainty but well-rounded figure. She talked in teen vernacular ("super" and "terrific" were the big

Shirley was always ready for a coke or a joke, except when she was looking into the camera.

Joseph Cotten treated his teenaged co-star as an adult, which won her gratitude and admiration.

The Conchita Rosita Juanita Lopez look wasn't quite right for the All-American girl.

Shirley never became a wartime pinup girl, despite the attempts of several photographers.

63

Springtime for Shirley in 1944 meant *I'll Be Seeing You*.

One of forty-two Westlake graduates in 1945, Shirley was the only one with Adrian shoulders padded into her white-lace gown, but like the other girls she carried a dozen pink roses.

David O. Selznick congratulates the most famous member of Westlake's Class of '45.

Shirley's class willed her "points off for misbehavior" record to Susie Tracy, Mr. and Mrs. Spencer Tracy's daughter.

65

words in 1945.) She asserted her own strong wll and began to resent, albeit mildly, some of the interference run for her by her mother and certain members of the Selznick organization. She pondered going to college (the University of California at Los Angeles) but decided to continue her studies under private tutors at the Selznick studio.

"I think I'll start by taking Spanish and psychology," she told a visitor, who then asked, "Why psychology?" A Selznick press agent interjected nervously: "That's difficult to answer. Why does anyone study psychology? It's like asking, 'Why do you like baseball?'" Shirley cut him off: "It's not anything of the kind," she snapped. "I'm interested in psychology because I want to know more about people. I've got to learn the psychology of being a wife anyway."

John Agar was Shirley's favorite serviceman, and first husband, 1945.

John and Shirley Agar's wedding reception was held in the Temple backyard, 1945.

66

All summer before her wedding, when she wasn't preparing for it, she hung around with her friends from school. She even visited Westlake. "It was fun, walking around like old grads," she said. She enjoyed dancing in the evening, wore inexpensive girlish clothes at home, played with her pet Pekinese and enjoyed the beach in Santa Monica. Shirley was giggly, but not gushy in the Hollywood manner; at the Selznick studios she was everybody's darling as she had been at 20th Century-Fox. But her crowd was never made up of filmland's "sophisticates" and she never called anyone "darling." Her makeup, even for public occasions, was conservative and subdued, especially for the postwar period: no eyeshadow, very little rouge and only a slight amount of lipstick.

Shirley planned to continue her career, at least

Flanked by Gertrude, George and John, Shirley waves good-bye before leaving on her honeymoon.

67

until John was discharged and they made decisions about his career and having children. Three weeks after her wedding she was in Denver for a victory bond benefit show appearance. John returned from the service and he and Shirley moved into their ten-room "cottage." He had thought at one time of joining the family meat-packing business in Chicago, but meeting and marrying Shirley had changed all that. While she shunned the glamourous social side of Hollywood, he loved the constant whirl of parties, restaurants and clubs. She still loved her drugstore ice-cream soda fountain, while he preferred drinking something stronger. For the first six months of the marriage, these differences hardly mattered, and the Selznick publicity machine, the columnists, Louella Parsons and Sheila Graham especially, told the world how happy Shirley and John Agar were.

Shirley's eighteenth birthday party, with John in beaming attendance, was given by RKO on the set of *Honeymoon*, a picture she was filming, on loanout from Selznick, with Franchot Tone and Guy Madison. Although the moviegoing public had been pummeled with incidents affirming Shirley's adulthood, from her first long dress and first screen kiss to her marriage, the party was billed as yet another entry into official adulthood. "Little Miss Marker is burning down the Little Red Schoolhouse and playing legal hooky for the first time," read the invitation for April 23, 1946, at 4 P.M. Shirley did burn down a replica of a little red schoolhouse for the 150 guests, who included former co-stars James Dunn, Jack Oakie and Adolphe Menjou. Hamburgers, hot dogs, salad and Cokes were served, and a band played.

A woman wearing a big placard labelled "Welfare Worker" and representing Shirley's studio tutors was run off the soundstage by a man dressed as "Father Time." Sailor Vincent, a well-known stuntman and longtime friend of Shirley's, brought in a phony paste birthday cake while the band played "Happy Birthday." He tripped in front of her and fell flat on his face in the cake. He then brought in a real cake with eighteen candles, and John helped Shirley blow them out.

At home Shirley and John were having less and less domestic bliss. Despite flurries of premature rumors to the contrary, the couple didn't have their first child until January 1948. Shirley was nineteen. The baby was named Linda Susan Agar (almost from the beginning she was called simply Susan) and before she was less than a month old Selznick tried to sign her for movies—in fact, he had tried to make the deal even before the child was born. The terms: $100 weekly for the first three years of the baby's life (without working), at which point Selznick would have an option on its services; in the case of twins, $200 a week. In February 1948, Selznick visited the Agars "to see the baby" but got nowhere. Shirley was determined that her daughter "Susie" should not be subjected to life as a child star.

The baby at least shored up the public image of the Agar marriage, and John himself turned out to be the new movie star in the family. He appeared with Shirley, John Wayne and Henry Fonda in John Ford's *Fort Apache* in 1948, and with her and Robert Young in 1949's *Adventure in Baltimore*. But he had no visible acting talent and naturally his earnings were far less than hers. He got tired of being "Mr. Shirley Temple," a consort to Hollywood's princess. He kept erratic hours and indulged in heavy drinking. They had frequent quarrels. He complained that her life was too ordered and told friends it was difficult to have any fun with Shirley. Because her life was ordered she wanted to stop short of breaking up her home and family, but she said John had driven her to the brink of suicide. After a six-day thinking period in Palm Springs, in October 1949, twenty-one-year-old Shirley Temple decided to sue twenty-eight-year-old John Agar for divorce, seeking no reparations but asking custody of Susan, then twenty months old.

She released the news in routine Hollywood style by telephoning columnist Louella Parsons. "It's not sudden," Shirley told Louella. "I didn't want to break up my home and my marriage, but there's no other way. I don't want to hurt John. I want our separation and divorce to be dignified. I am merely going to charge cruelty. John is a nice boy, but he's a little mixed up. The worst thing about all this is what it will do to the baby." To Sheilah Graham, a Louella rival, Shirley said, "The trouble with my marriage started two and a half years ago, when Johnny started to drink. My suit doesn't mention drinking, but it has become unbearable."

Agar said he was going home to his mother and announced he was not going to contest the divorce, which Shirley filed only on the grounds of mental cruelty. "I agree with Shirley that it

Sequins, rayon and heavy red lipstick were the 1940s idea of glamour.

No, Shirley, we already have a Rita Hayworth.

Not only was she not too young for strapless formals, Shirley was married and pregnant in 1947.

John Agar and his new bride were all smiles for a couple of years.

At the age of three months, Linda Susan Agar made her debut before the still cameras, with John and Shirley in strictly supporting roles, 1948.

must be done in a dignified manner," he said, adding when asked why he wasn't fighting back, "my shoulders are big enough."

Hollywood tended to take Shirley's side in the split. She was after all the bigger star, and a likable, friendly and sensible young lady. After ruling that Agar's share of community property be put in trust for Susan, the judge who granted Shirley's decree remarked: "This plaintiff occupies a place in the hearts and affections of the country, and the failure of her marriage was a distressing disappointment to many people." This time Shirley really had become an adult publicly, and to ease her distress, the judge restored her maiden name of Shirley Temple.

In later years, Shirley would only say of her first marriage: "My husband was twenty-four when we married and became an actor after we got married. But this turned out to be a poor decision. I would say that neither one of us was ready for marriage at that time. And so it did not work out. But the one bit of philosophy I learned then—and I still use it—is to give yourself another chance. You've always heard of other people giving you another break. I believe in do-it-yourself too. I was married a second time and it's a magnificent marriage."

Even before the breakup of her marriage to Agar, Shirley's career had gone into a rapid decline. While none of her later pictures, from 1947–49, actually lost money, she wasn't setting box-office records either, and the films had a cheapie "B" look about them and indifferent performances from her. Selznick, who still held her contract, suggested, not very gently, that after the divorce Shirley should go to Italy with her daughter and study acting, and even possibly take a different name. She had been fatally typed, he said, and her career was going nowhere. As proof of that he told Shirley that he had suggested her for a part in a film to be directed by Carol Reed (who was later to be knighted and to win an Oscar for *Oliver!*). Reed had replied sneeringly, and called her a "little bon-bon with a candy smile who couldn't act and had no character." Never one to be self-deluded, Shirley admitted that there had been "none of the pictures in the grown-up period that I'm really proud of," and she quit the movies once again, this time for good. She was twenty-one years old.

Her marriage and career absolutely ended,

This Junior Mrs. publicity shot was a portent of the suburban matron Shirley Temple Agar Black was to become.

Shirley took off, in January 1950—not for Italy but Hawaii. She took her daughter and her mother and father by clipper airplane, and the foursome settled into a rented house near Diamond Head on Oahu, presumably for a two-week stay. Shirley brooded about her life situation, while her old friends in the islands gave a round of parties for the trim and glamorous ex-movie star. The guest lists always included a number of single and attractive young men, invited in an effort to cheer her up. Shirley was only half grateful. "I didn't like men at all, at that point," she recalled.

The plot then became even soapier than some of her movies. A tall (compared to her), dark, handsome, rich and social young stranger walked into her life. He had skipped two of the parties for Shirley—to go surfing—but Charles Alden Black of San Francisco managed to make it to a third one. "It's corny," Shirley recalled, "but, you know, 'Some Enchanted Evening . . . across a crowded room.'" Black further endeared himself to the guest of honor by first mistaking her for a secretary working in Honolulu (normal American young womanhood at last!) and then admitting that he had never seen a Shirley Temple movie.

Black was thirty years old, having been born in Oakland, California, on March 6, 1919. He had gone to Hotchkiss, Harvard and the Stanford business school, and his father was James B. Black, president and later chairman of Pacific Gas and Electric Company, the largest private utility company in the world. Reputedly one of the richest young men in California, Charles Black had been a naval officer in World War II, was awarded the U.S. Navy's Silver Star, and had twice been cited for bravery in the Pacific. He was in Hawaii in 1950 as assistant to the president of Hawaiian Pineapple.

The instant romance between Charles and Shirley forced her two-week stay to extend to a month and a half, and in tears Shirley finally left Honolulu in mid-March "sort of engaged"—although her divorce from Agar would not be final until December of that year. Later in March Black resigned from the pineapple company and moved back to San Francisco. In April, Louella Parsons heard the story, and broke it first on her Sunday radio show, then in her Monday column. Shirley, vacationing with her parents in Del Monte, California, denied that there was any engagement, but she did go up to San Francisco later in April to attend The Bachelor's Ball with Charles Black.

It turned out to be his last Bachelor's Ball, because when her divorce decree became final, Charles and Shirley were married, on December 16, 1950, at his parents' home in Monterey. The whole Black family were avid in their dislike of publicity, never wanting to be photographed, much less interviewed, and Charles was no exception. Thus the press didn't find out about Shirley's second marriage until after her quiet second honeymoon at Cypress Point. (Being married to a former film star had a second disadvantage apart from publicity: Charles was dropped from the Social Register.)

Charles had taken a job with television station KTTV in Los Angeles, and the Blacks and Susan, who was legally adopted by her stepfather, moved into a house in Bel-Air. But because of the Korean War, in April 1951 Charles was recalled into the Navy as a Lieutenant Commander, and assigned to Washington, D.C. In leaving the Bel-Air house Shirley had to deal with her doll collection, then numbering 740 dolls and insured for $30,000. She decided to lend the collection to the State of California for five years, and they were placed on display at the State Exposition Building in Los Angeles.

There were original Ravca (French) dolls with silk stocking faces and dolls made of dried apples, whose constantly forming mold had to be cleaned away. The smallest doll was made of china and measured one and a half inches high; the largest was the Japanese bride she had been given in Hawaii. Other dolls represented Gainsborough's "Blue Boy" and Lawrence's "Pinky," and various countries of the world: Mexico, Ireland, Germany, and French Indo-China. A section of the exhibit was devoted to nursery tales: the Old Woman Who Lived in a Shoe, and the Three Little Pigs. Bill Robinson had given his protegee a carved wooden doll in his likeness, complete with a movable face, a derby hat and the ability to whistle, and it was on display along with dolls representing "The Spirit of '76." To round out the exhibit there were several dolls that looked like Shirley Temple.

Crossing the continent by car Charles was forced to leave Shirley and Susan in Tulsa, Oklahoma, because Shirley's appendix had to be removed. She eventually joined him in a cozy walk-up apartment on Wyoming Avenue off Connecticut Avenue in the District, behind an old building in which Vice President Alben Barkley, among others, had lived. Shirley's near-journalistic curiosity attracted her to a U.S.S.R. office building across the street from the flat; she spent days in rapt but unproductive casing of it.

"I loved Washington," she recalled. "It has such a small-town air about it. Everyone whispers and looks so important. I was pregnant most of the time, or so it seemed. When I look at pictures of myself at Embassy parties I get bigger and bigger and bigger." At the suggestion of a top naval officer Shirley decided to have her baby at Bethesda Naval Hospital to help wartime morale. Charles Alden Black, Jr. was born there on April 28, 1952, but complications following the Caesarean birth briefly threatened Shirley's life. Although her illness was covered by the nation's press, Shirley had caught some of her husband's publicity-shyness: the first photographs of Charles Jr. weren't released until he was seven months old.

The Blacks bought a house on fashionable River Road in Bethesda, Maryland, to escape downtown Washington's summer heat. The house was in a rustic setting with four acres of land. Shirley would borrow her neighbor's tractor and, wearing a scarf like any contemporary housewife, ride it around to survey her holdings—only to have tourists ask her to move out of the way so they could take photographs of Shirley Temple's house. She picked wild flowers for her husband until they discovered his frequent sneezing was from the local ragweed, unknown in his native California. Shirley herself suffered a severe case of chicken pox in 1952. (When Susan asked her once what she had missed in her childhood, Shirley replied: "Darling, only the mumps!" Those came later in adulthood, too, in 1955—on both sides.)

Louis Parsons, a vice president of United States Steel, took the Blacks under his wing socially. They attended and gave small dinner parties where government officials and foreign diplomats discussed the Cold War, Korea, nuclear armaments, the economy, the United Nations and the future of the world, and the Blacks were invited to, and attended, various embassy functions. For Shirley this represented a whole new area of interest, although Charles had long been interested in politics and world affairs. Both, as Republicans, got even more into the government mainstream after the election of Dwight Eisenhower to the Presidency in November 1952, and his inauguration in January 1953. "During the two years we were in Washington, I had meant to get involved only in local politics," Shirley recalled. "After all, I was finally old enough to vote. But of course in

In the mid-1950s Robert Wagner was one of Hollywood's new faces, while Shirley Temple Black, mother of three, was its fading past. They chatted during a dinner honoring Darryl F. Zanuck.

Charles and Shirley had met in Hawaii and often returned there for vacations, as they did in 1957. *Credit: Harry Redl for LIFE.*

Charles Black married Shirley in 1950. Seven years later they were back in California, having lived in Washington, and she was plunging into civic work as a prelude to politics.

Washington local politics are national and international politics."

Charles was discharged from the Navy after the war and the Blacks were free to move back to Los Angeles in May 1953. There he worked as business manager of another television station, KABC-TV. On April 9, 1954, Shirley's second daughter and third child, Lori Alden Black, was born at Santa Monica Hospital, where Shirley had also been born. The same nurse who attended Shirley's birth and later Susan's was rebooked for Lori's debut, which was also accomplished by Caesarean section.

From time to time Shirley was approached to do television and movie work, and even to act on stage, something she'd never done. "I worked for eighteen years," she said in declining the offers, "that's long enough. My only contract is a marriage contract, and my only role is motherhood," she added. Even Selznick asked her to come back, to do a part in the Thomas A. Edison Centennial television show, and she was tempted. "I accepted on the telephone," she remembered, "and then little Charlie got sick and I called back and said 'I guess I'm too much of a mother.' But I would have done it if I had only realized that my father-in-law's company was one of the sponsors."

In September 1954 Charles became director of business operations for the Stanford University Research Institute, and the Blacks moved once again, to Atherton, twenty-eight miles south of San Francisco. Atherton was an aggressively upwardly mobile, upper-middle-class area that contained some fancy estates with gates and long drives, and one-acre subdivisions. The Blacks chose a plain, beige-colored, one-story California ranch-style house with five bedrooms on a tree-lined cul-de-sac. Shirley decorated the house herself, and until she undertook a television series in late 1957 also did all the cooking, confining her paid help to a once-a-week cleaning woman. "My taste is very conservative," she avowed. "I'm drawn to Oriental things but I don't think one can have many unless the house is to be all Oriental."

And so she mixed together her ancient Tibetan scroll, American Oriental furniture and carriage lamps from the gates of the Bethesda house. The entrance hall featured a six-foot by two-foot bed of pure white pebbles in which sat glass net floats and bottles Shirley and Charles had scavenged

Susan, Charles Jr. and Lori Black picnicked on the patio in Atheron while their suburban mom arranged daisies, summer 1957.

Mrs. Black in 1957, preparing to do her storybook TV show, watches herself as *Rebecca of Sunnybrook Farm* from twenty years before. *Credit: Phil Stern for LIFE.*

from Hawaii's beaches. On a green cement patio out back Charles built an L-shaped rock garden with a fountain and a Buddha statue. Shirley planted birds-of-paradise even though she had been told they wouldn't grow in northern California (they did for her) and roses and bamboos off the patio.

Hollywood was represented by the bookcase behind the living room piano, where in a neat row reddish-brown leather albums were lined up, with the title of one of Shirley's movies lettered in gold on each. The albums contained stills from, and clippings about, the films. (The Blacks also kept a leather album for each year of their marriage, most containing photographs taken by Charles.) And although Shirley swore that none of her children would be subjected to show business until they were adults and chose it for themselves, their bedrooms were full of Shirley Temple touches. In Lori's room there was a screen decorated with pictures of little Shirley, and the Christmas that Lori was three, Santa Claus gave her a Shirley Temple doll. In Charlie's room a photograph of Mom as moppet hung on one wall, and Susan, like her mother before her, had what looked like a doll factory for a bedroom and what most people would consider far too many toys.

Other than indulging their children, the Blacks were not interested in conspicuous consumption, and for independently wealthy people lived way below their means. They owned two cars, but both were Chevrolets, one a station wagon, the other a convertible. Shirley had to work a little harder at being a suburbanite—or "exurbanite" as she preferred it—than most of the neighborhood women. But she accomplished it gracefully and determinedly played the role of wife next door for a while.

She was active in several charity groups, mostly ones involved in helping children. Although a member of the Peninsula Children's Theatre (which brought low-cost live theatre to young audiences) she was never asked to act by them, even when the group did *Heidi*. "I guess I'm not the type," she sighed, "but I knew something about that one." So instead she ushered, painted scenery, and served as hospitality and publicity chairman. In the latter capacity she sent identical releases to all the local newspapers; no one printed them. She tried "exclusives" and one San Francisco paper wrote back asking her please to double space, put her name, address, organization's name and phone number in the upper left-hand corner, and use fewer than eight carbons.

Every Monday Shirley put on a smock to sell goods at the Allied Arts Guild, which supported a children's convalescent home. She worked for a rehabilitation center for crippled children and adults. When her brother George developed muscular dystrophy, she went to work for the national organization to combat the disease.

Charles changed jobs again in 1957 and became director of corporate relations for the Ampex Corporation in nearby Redwood City. He and Shirley went into San Francisco ("the city") only about once every two weeks, but they did see friends in the neighborhood a few times a week. In 1954 both joined the conservationist Sierra Club and began their long-standing involvement in the problems of ecology. They went on picnics near the ocean with the children, and took to rock hunting. Shirley liked to snorkel and Charles favored skin diving. Both played golf, with her score ranging from 100 to 125 for eighteen holes. They went to bed and got up early, and once all the kids were at least in nursery school life was, in Shirley's words, "very quiet and very nice."

Comebacks in any field are tricky and are therefore usually carefully mulled over and plotted before being attempted. Those in show business involving a change of medium—and dependent on a fickle public—are especially so. After her comeback in films, starting with some promise and fizzling into a lack of creativity on her part and total indifference on the audience's, Shirley certainly had no desire to try motion pictures ever again. But television (still largely in its "live" phase in the late 1950s) was still new enough to seem fascinating and challenging. Shirley's children, like most other Americans, adored TV, although their parents strictly controlled their selection of programs and limited their total viewing time.

The three Black children saw very few movies, even their mother's. When Susan saw her first Shirley Temple film, *Rebecca of Sunnybrook Farm*, her five-year-old's critique was "Mommy, you didn't sing very well." Told that her mother as Rebecca was pretending to have lost her voice in that portion of the film, Susan repeated: "You still didn't sing very well." "I used to show my movies to the children when they were little," Shirley recalled. "I thought I had a neat opportunity at their birthday parties. That worked with each child beautifully until about age seven. Then they said, 'Can't we go to the roller rink or do something besides seeing one of those old films?'"

Television was a different story. Although she had been consistent in her refusal to consider TV offers from 1950–57 and "concentrated totally on being a housewife and mother—and of course a born volunteer"—the proposal for "Shirley Temple's Storybook" was something else. After all, "as a child I lived in a storybook world; it was like living in books instead of just reading them. I *was* Heidi in Switzerland, Wee Willie Winkie in India, the Little Princess in England, and I got to sit on Abraham Lincoln's knee. Imagine a little girl being allowed to dress up in those wonderful Civil War costumes, with pantalettes and hoop skirts! Nothing was impossible and it all seemed real. How can any of us, however grown up, deny the importance of make-believe in our lives?" she asked. "Aren't all of us living and working for things that we hope will come true?"

Henry Jaffe had been executive producer of Dinah Shore's live television variety show and a producer of "Producer's Showcase," a well-mounted series of TV spectaculars begun in 1953. He had had particular success in the latter with productions of *Peter Pan* and *Jack and the Bean-stalk* and wanted to do a whole series of fairy tales for TV. Jaffe was accidentally seated next to Shirley Temple Black in March 1957 at a testimonial dinner in his honor given by AFTRA, the radio and television actors' union. Nervous about the occasion, Jaffe had a headache, couldn't eat and could barely speak. He gaspingly requested an aspirin from Shirley. "I've never been sick a day in my life," she exaggerated, explaining why she didn't have one. "I felt terrible," Jaffe recalled, "particularly when I had to make a speech. I could hardly stand. But little Shirley helped me up and practically held me there."

The brief encounter led Jaffe to choose Shirley as the hostess-narrator of his fairy-tale series, quickly titled "Shirley Temple's Storybook." He sent his associate, Alvin Cooperman, to Atherton to see her. "I told Shirley what we had in mind and she seemed to know immediately how we wanted it done," Cooperman recalled. "It was just the kind of show she approved of, and we just sat there and talked it over." To his surprise, Shirley was so sure she wanted to do it (and Charles Sr. had voiced the family's consensus: "It might be nice") that "she got out her typewriter and we worked out a one-page contract. Shirley didn't have an agent and she laughingly suggested maybe she should call her lawyers. But she didn't. When the one page sounded right to her, she just sat right down and signed it, on the bridge table in her living room."

Later the contract was redone by Shirley's lawyers. It got longer, but didn't contain anything of substance that Shirley hadn't already included in the one-page draft. "I'm a lawyer," marveled Jaffe. "But if I needed a lawyer, I'd take Shirley." "I think it's because Shirley is interested in everything that is going on around her," added Cooperman. "So naturally she'd be interested in business too."

Priorities had solidly shifted in Shirley's "third life," in as many decades of show business. Now home and family in Atherton were clearly top priority, and work for the first time was something she merely dabbled in. The sixteen "Storybook" shows were done over the course of three years, and Shirley commuted to Hollywood. "It's funny, having to go to the Beverly Hills Hotel in your own city," she said, "to get a good night's sleep before you can get into a work mood." She also found that in the new career there would be competition: only the strong survived the Nielsen ratings. On the other hand, as a child "I was never competitive. I never had to work very hard because there weren't many little girls working."

During the "Storybook" phase of her life, at ages twenty-nine through thirty-two and at a trim 107 pounds on her five-foot-two frame, looking far more attractive than the matronly image she was projecting on screen and off, Shirley was already putting distance between herself and "the little girl." She ran into another star of her early childhood, now making a TV comeback, too, on the soundstages of Screen Gems–Columbia where she was working: Rin-Tin-Tin. "I class myself with Rin-Tin-Tin," she said. "In the Depression people were looking for something to cheer them up. They fell in love with a dog—and with a little girl. It won't happen again."

She refused to draw on the little girl for her "Storybook" work. "I feel like she's a relative of mine," said the adult Shirley, "yet I'm sort of detached and critical." And on TV she certainly wouldn't be singing any of little Shirley's familiar songs, least of all, "On the Good Ship Lollipop." "I got awfully tired of singing that even as a kid," she explained. "I simply was asked to sing it too many times."

There were two further forays into television after the March 1961 filming of the last "Shirley Temple Storybook," which was shown later that year. In April 1963, Shirley arrived at CBS Television City in Hollywood to tape an hour-long segment of "The Red Skelton Show." It wasn't yet another comeback, she insisted, but she hinted at some future show business plans and said, "Fortunately, I can work when I want to." During the approximately forty minutes of the show in which she was involved, Shirley sang "By the Beautiful Sea" and a few bars of "Side by Side" with Skelton, and in a "Freddy the Freeloader" sketch entitled "Passion in Pasadena" she played a very rich girl.

Her star-power was still such that a steady stream of performers from other productions, CBS executives, studio workers and their children trooped through the Skelton set the four days Shirley was working, to meet her and get her autograph. It was highly unusual; most other stars were treated in a more blase fashion. The show's crew found her, as all her other crews before them had, highly professional, unaffected and coolly friendly. The show's choreographer noted that "all the dancers liked her—and this can be unusual for dancers. She was a star from the time they made real stars." The crew noticed that Skelton held back his usual ribald antics during Shirley's appearance because she seemed so poised and ladylike. "I don't think he was comfortable," recalled one stage hand, "but he certainly didn't act like he did when Martha Raye was here."

Shirley's rehearsals started on a Saturday, with the actual taping to take place the following Tuesday, April 23, her thirty-fifth birthday. She had celebrated with Charles and the children at home in Woodside, where they had moved from nearby Atherton in 1961, before her arrival in Hollywood, where she spent four nights alone in a hotel, even having her dinner in her room. "I never saw old friends when I went to Hollywood to work," she said.

Shirley was a little stiff during rehearsals, but on taping day, her birthday, she loosened up into some Skelton-style clowning. A long loaf of French bread was used in the sketch, and for two days Red had been chewing on it between rehearsals. During a scene in which Shirley got married to the other man and Skelton was supposed to be in tears, she whipped a half loaf of the bread out from under her wedding gown and started munching, breaking him up.

A reminiscent birthday cake, large enough to feed over a hundred, was wheeled onto the set for Shirley's party. She recalled that she could be only thirty-four if she wanted to, thanks to her parents and 20th Century-Fox. "It was quite a shock to be told at what I thought was my twelfth birthday, that I was actually thirteen," she recalled. "I hadn't prepared to be a teenager." Charles, Susan, Charles Jr. and Lori all sent telegrams on Mom's thirty-fifth, but "I never did get supper on my birthday because I took the hour break during taping to fix my make-up and hair. I ended up by eating two bananas in my hotel room by myself at ten o'clock that night." The show must go on.

At the turn of the new year 1965, Shirley did a TV pilot, written especially for her. It was filmed at her old studio, 20th Century-Fox, which was rapidly becoming more of a production center for television shows than for motion pictures. The name of the show was "Go Fight City Hall," and it was a half-hour pilot for the American Broadcasting Company television network, a situation comedy about a young social worker. Shirley was supposed to work for the Department of Public Assistance and play a do-gooder who kept getting into trouble. Her co-stars were Bill Hayes and Jack Kruschen. Had it been successful, the full series of shows would have gone into production in May 1965, and Shirley was promised she could finish her work by September.

She was still insisting that the role she was best suited for was "wife and mother" and that she had had to get the consent of her husband and all her children to undertake the project. After Susan graduated from high school in June, the plan was to take a house on the ocean in Santa Monica or Malibu for the summer, for Shirley and the children. To make the pilot she once again commuted the 400 miles from Woodside. Shirley said on embarking on the series that she felt there was a great need for social workers, and "I'm hopeful that the show will create strong interest among young people, particularly women, to go into this line of work." It never had a chance to, as the network, after seeing the pilot, refused to buy the full series. Ten years later Shirley said, "I really didn't like the idea; I'm glad it never got off the ground."

Still, the pilot itself was an event in the Hollywood tradition. "Welcome Home, Shirley" proclaimed a huge banner furled across the 20th Century-Fox Studio gate. And there was a champagne lunch in the commissary with old friends and studio executives. Still a resident schoolteacher on the lot, Shirley's tutor, Frances Klampt ("Klammie") was at the lunch. Shirley recalled that she had celebrated several birthdays in this studio commissary, and that when she had left Fox aged twelve she had left all her baby teeth behind. "My very nice bungalow is now the studio hospital," she noted. "I don't know if there's a message in that or not. If I had kept digging in the ground behind the bungalow I might have struck oil before Fox did."

Marriage at its best," said Shirley Temple Black, "should never limit a woman who wants to and must keep growing, continue her education and widen her scope." For Shirley, ever since she had entered that prep-school race to see who would be the first girl in her class to the altar (and won

On her thirty-fifth birthday, in 1963, Shirley guested on Red Skelton's show but had a hard time loosening up.

it, but lost at the same time), "it was very important to have a husband." On the other hand, she had begun working for a living at age three and had established an indelible separate identity through that work; being Shirley Temple was quite independent of who her husband was. Indeed, it didn't matter whether or not she had a husband at all—to the public, that is. To her it mattered a lot.

Fortunately, in Charles Black Shirley had "the kind of husband who pushes me out the door. He likes me to get involved. He urges me on. But he also lets me make my own decisions." Charles and Shirley had mutual and long-standing interests in ecology and the law of the sea. And, especially after he founded and became president of the Mardela Corporation, which was involved in marine instrument resource development, "aquaculture"—methods to get food from the seas: fish, algae and seaweed—and she became involved in the United Nations, Charles and Shirley's working lives paralleled. "We've always been on the same track," she explained. "That's why we have such a good marriage."

While Charles certainly encouraged her to get involved in politics, international affairs and diplomacy, Shirley was strong-willed enough to want to make her own way. And, in the seventeen years from 1960, when she was still a show-business bubblehead, to 1977 when she was recognized throughout the world as a serious, hardworking former United States Ambassador to Ghana and U.S. Chief of Protocol, she did just that.

"Children should be older before a woman starts a career in public life," Shirley said in explaining why she hadn't plunged into elective or appointive politics before her race for Congress in 1967. She had been actively interested in the Republican Party since her Washington years of the early 1950s, and one of the last things Shirley had done before returning to California in 1953 was to meet the new Vice President of the United States, a fellow Californian and former senator, Richard M. Nixon. It wasn't until the 1960 Presidential election, however, that she got personally involved. As a volunteer, Shirley was precinct captain for Nixon in his race against John F. Kennedy, and with hundreds of other Republican women of San Mateo County she worked stuffing envelopes, walking precincts, and getting out the

vote. Nixon won the county and California, but lost the election. Shirley wasn't discouraged, even after Lyndon Johnson defeated Barry Goldwater in 1964.

She began to accept fund-raising rallies and speaking engagements on behalf of the Party, many of them out of state. At the Texas Republican Party's state central committee meeting in Houston in early 1967, she talked of "all of us ordinary citizens getting involved. I so believed that speech," she said, "that I decided to run for Congress when it looked like Representative J. Arthur Younger would be too ill to run again." Younger, a Republican who had represented the generally conservative San Mateo 11th Congressional District for twelve years, died suddenly in June. The previous Easter Sunday he had encouraged Shirley to make the race, saying, "I won't be around forever." "We didn't know he was as ill as he was," Shirley recalled. But she took Younger's imprimatur, and the advice of former co-stars George Murphy (*Little Miss Broadway*) and Ronald Reagan (*That Hagen Girl*), who by then were, respectively, the Republican Senator from, and Governor of, California and declared for Congress.

"Little Shirley Temple is not running for anything," she told a press conference in the Polynesian-style private dining room of Villa Chartier, a San Mateo motel restaurant on August 29, 1967. "If someone insists on pinning me with a label, make it read Shirley Temple Black, Republican independent." Reagan had set the special off-year election to fill the vacant seat for November 14, making Shirley's entry dangerously late. She joined a previously listed male field of eleven candidates, three other Republicans and eight Democrats. If none of the twelve achieved a majority vote, a run-off would be held between the top Republican and the top Democrat a month later (although all candidates were listed without party identification on the original ballot).

In an atmosphere more conducive to a Junior League brunch, Shirley, wearing a boxy apricot-colored suit with a long carcoat and a jade necklace, explained to the press and a cheering claque of her own supporters why she, a thirty-nine-year-old housewife and ex-movie star, should be sent to Congress. She faced the battery of still and television cameras like the pro that she was, dimpled frequently and demanded to be taken

(Opposite page) A beaming mother helps Susan get ready for a deb ball in San Francisco, 1965. *Credit: Alfred Eisenstadt for LIFE.*

The roses were red when Susan graduated from high school, in 1965, twenty years after her mother had. *Credit: Alfred Eisenstadt for LIFE.*

In 1967 Shirley Temple Black came in second in a field of eleven for a seat in Congress from San Mateo County. It wasn't any of the seven Democrats who beat her, it was one of her three fellow Republicans pictured here—Paul ("Pete") McCloskey, on her immediate left.
Credit: Fred Kaplan, Black Star.

seriously. She attacked President Lyndon B. Johnson for having "played politics with the Vietnam War and with the riots" and she reached back to her youth for the most crushing of metaphors: "the Great Society, a pretty bad movie in the first place, has become a Great Flop," she said.

Shirley said she wanted to do her share "to help solve some of the critical problems which face the nation today and get the country back on the road to progress. It is not progress for the largest, strongest military power in the world to be mired down in an apparently endless war with one of the smallest and weakest countries in the world. It is not progress when some of our citizens participate in bloody riots and burn down whole sections of cities. It is not progress when pornography becomes big business and when our children are exposed to it. It is not progress when some of our young people are so uninspired by our present leadership that they reject society,

turn to drugs and become so-called 'hippies'."

Three attractive peninsula matrons, Shirley's colleagues for thirteen years of charity work, passed out copies of her statement and led a group of mothers and daughters in cheering and applause so excitedly that one member of the press got to the floor and said, "This is no rally, this is a press conference. Who are these people anyway?" "I don't know," smiled Shirley, "but I'm awfully glad to see them here." Another questioner wanted to know if she was a dove on Vietnam, given her statement. "I'm a mother with a fifteen-year-old son, but we do have to honor our commitment there," she hedged, "to prevent communism from taking over. But the job has to be done quickly and LBJ should rely on the Joint Chiefs of Staff for his military advice rather than on McNamara; I don't know what should be done militarily, I'm not a military man."

As the third former film star to seek office as a

California Republican in the last three years, Shirley was asked if she thought actors without political experience were justified in seeking national political careers. "Not all movie actors should be in politics," she agreed. "But then, all haberdashers shouldn't be in politics either," she added, recalling Harry Truman. And as for Congress specifically, "no one is experienced in Congress until he gets there," she said. Her qualifications were that she was "an honest, hard-working woman who will do an honest job. I have lived here over thirteen years; people know what I've been doing since I was three." Charles, whose father had become a member of Reagan's Committee on Efficiency in Government, was standing at the back of the room. He said that if Shirley won the special election the whole family would go with her to Washington, D.C.

Shirley's position on virtually all issues of the day was vague and waffling. On the civil riots then seemingly sweeping America in black ghettos, she said "We have to stop thinking of each other as being of different colors—we are all Americans. We must have real equality in this country, and the responsibility that goes with it. I'm for anything that will make life better for all Americans. But these people, the Negroes, have been let down. Tremendous promises have been made by the Administration. I feel we need more vocational education and we need to give people suffering in riot areas a sense of meaningful achievement."

The Congressional campaign itself was like no other in American history. "Shirley You Jest" read a popular bumper sticker for Republicans and Democrats alike. But Shirley Black wasn't jesting. "No one really asked me any questions," she recalled of the 1967 race. "During that campaign Vietnam was just about the only thing discussed. They didn't ask me how I felt about the People's Republic of China, which I was even then, in my way, trying to get into the United Nations. They didn't ask me about lowering the voting age to eighteen, about which I had spoken all over the country. But I wasn't asked questions that really said what I was."

Although a campaign aide conceded that either Shirley or Charles could have written out a check for the entire cost of her campaign, Shirley insisted on raising the money in more usual political style, by contributions from other organizations and individuals. But by entering so late, long after the

other serious candidates had their financing, she was prevented from conducting the kind of campaign at which she clearly would have excelled: television "messages." As it was, she could manage only two thirty-second spots and one one-minute spot, because to reach the small San Mateo constituency it was necessary to buy commercials for the entire San Francisco Bay area, most of whose voters couldn't vote for her. Shirley was offered free exposure on the ninety-minute Jim Dunbar television show before the election, but a strike was on at the station and she wouldn't cross the picket line. "I have never crossed a picket line in my life and I wasn't about to start then. I would do it again today," she said after she became Ambassador. "I still wouldn't cross the picket line. But even at that, if the campaign had been two weeks longer I could have won."

She was forced, therefore, in "the very clever political campaign against me," to rely on more intimate techniques, such as standing outside of factories shaking hands, and meeting men and women at small gatherings "where they would decide as couples." Razzle-dazzle entered into the race, and Democrat Roy Archibald, a San Mateo city councilman and former mayor, used his World War II PT-boat skipper experience like President Kennedy's to give his campaign the image: "PT-453 versus The Good Ship Lollipop."

A formal debate requested by one of the other Democrats to make his campaign stand out—the format was popular from the Nixon–Kennedy race and Shirley was thought to be the logical opponent to use to get attention—was held at the El Camino High School gymnasium, shortly before the election. Three other Democrats were included, at Shirley's insistence, but she was the only Republican. "I am only concerned at conserving party unity," she said with a wicked grin when asked why she had not invited the others to attend. The evening was clearly orchestrated as a showcase for Shirley.

Wearing a red suit and an overabundance of lipstick, she arrived on Charles's arm. Her supporters were already there in full force, dancing about in red, white and blue sashes and carrying signs showing a matronly portrait of their candidate. Red balloons with Shirley's picture on them were handed out; a few were popped by little boys supporting one of the other candidates. The four Democrats got only a smattering of applause, while Shirley was wildly cheered as she settled herself on the right-hand side of the podium, under "HOME" on the basketball scoreboard. The four Democrats huddled on the left, and the moderator announced that he was "the only neutral person they could find—I'm from Berkeley" (outside the district).

Shirley started off with a fifteen-minute speech; each Democrat was allowed ten minutes. Then Shirley rebutted, then each Democrat rebutted. Three local newsmen filed on stage and asked questions—almost all of Shirley—and the candidates were allowed a brief reply to the questions. Candidates were not allowed to ask questions of each other and no one from the thousand people in the audience was supposed to speak.

After her opening spiel about coming out of private life to represent "the forgotten decent people of the country," Shirley made a remark that stunned even her own supporters. "How can you say 'stop the bombing of North Vietnam' when you can make a case that it hasn't even started?" she asked. After an uproar in the hall, she went on to advocate "a swift and honorable conclusion" to the war. One Democrat, Edward Keating, who followed her, said that Mrs. Black was "more to be pitied than censured" and that he and she lived in two different worlds if she thought the bombing had scarcely begun. Another, Andrew Baldwin, called Shirley "not a dove, not a hawk, but a blackbird." Archibald warned of escalation and counter-escalation and World War III.

Dan Monaco, who had organized the "debate," thanked Mrs. Black for being allowed to be present at her meeting; Shirley smiled tightly. She tried to recoup in the question period by saying that she was not, after all, for increased bombing nor for escalation of the war. She was for, naturally, freedom, justice, dignity, honor, friendship and a return to honesty and integrity in government. But it was too late. The voters of her affluent, highly-educated district saw through her shallow preparations for public office, and while she had thousands of fans in San Mateo County, less than twenty-seven percent of the electorate wanted her to represent them in Congress.

Ironically, it was none of the Democrats, but fellow Republican independent, Paul (Pete) McCloskey, who beat her in the special election, largely on the basis of his doveish stand on the Vietnam War. He went on to represent the district for several more full terms, and in 1972 ran in some Republican primaries for President against Nixon, on an anti-war platform. "I'm most proud that I came in second out of twelve," Shirley said. But I wish I could have represented the people of San Mateo county. I think it might have been better for them."

In the Presidential election of 1968 Shirley repressed her disappointment at her own defeat in the Congressional race and heavily involved herself in the national Republican campaign. Even before the candidates, Richard Nixon and Spiro Agnew, were selected, she made 200 speeches around the United States, coordinated by the Republican National Committee; she visited forty-six cities in twenty-two states. After the convention picked the Nixon–Agnew ticket, Shirley headed an effort to organize American voters living abroad and herself barnstormed nine foreign countries on behalf of Nixon.

"It was a nonpartisan vote drive," she explained. "But obviously we concentrated on likely Republicans. I got the idea from Clare Booth Luce; anyone can do it, it's just whoever thinks of it first." Absentee ballots from abroad went heavily for Nixon–Agnew, who just managed to squeak by at home, and Shirley had established herself as an appealing vote getter, at least for other Republicans. Her speeches raised more than $1 million. And her reward was not long in coming. In 1969 Nixon appointed Shirley Temple Black a United States delegate to the United Nations, for the international organization's twenty-fourth General Assembly.

There was ample precedent for an entertainer in the U.S. delegation to the U.N. (Marian Anderson, Irene Dunne and Myrna Loy had preceded Shirley to the post), which made her limited international experience slightly less offensive to critics. She had been co-founder of, and was currently international chairman of volunteers for, the International Federation of Multiple Sclerosis Societies. "I call the Federation my little U.N.," she explained, "and our secretariat is in Vienna." (In 1969, nineteen countries with Multiple Sclerosis organizations were members; in 1977 it was twenty-four.)

It was on a European trip to set up branches of the Federation—and incidentally to stump for Nixon—that Shirley had found herself besieged in a hotel room in Prague on the day, August 20, 1968, that Soviet troops took over Czechoslovakia. Fearing arrest, imprisonment or the firing squad,

Shirley tore a picture of deposed Czech president Alexander Dubcek into bits and flushed it down the toilet. She, along with four hundred other Americans, was later allowed to leave the country by car. "I think of this occurrence every year on August 20th," she recalled. "And it was on August 20, 1974, that President Ford named me Ambassador to Ghana."

When she arrived in New York in September 1969 to take her seat at the U.N. as the only woman on the five-person American delegation, Shirley carried a vivid red patent leather briefcase decorated with a blue "N" for Nixon—a souvenir of the victorious election the year before. Many of her countrymen, in and out of the U.N., greeted her appointment with smiles and snickers of derision and disbelief. Delegates and workers at the U.N. from other countries sought her out to get her autograph, "but I asked for all of theirs back," she recalled. "Everyone at the U.N. is a celebrity for about three days, but then you have to see who gets down to work. The delegates are about the best their countries can send, especially from Africa. They are so well-educated and so young—but they have to be, their countries are."

The slightly cool and distant receiving-line smile she began to develop as a child greeting prominent visitors to 20th Century-Fox served Shirley well at the endless round of U.N. embassy cocktail parties, and she quickly became a popular figure. Threatening letters from a man who said he would kill her forced her to have a bodyguard (a New York City Police detective paid for by the U.N.) with her at all times in New York—but even a bodyguard was something she had once been used to. Shirley lived alone in a luxury suite at the Barclay Hotel; the thirteen weeks of the General Assembly session, despite Charles's several visits and her frequent weekend flights to Woodside, represented the longest stretch of time she had lived apart from any of her families.

One night in the suite, as she was writing a letter to Charles, a creature she took to be a mouse brushed up against her leg. Shirley called the hotel operator and said "there's a black mouse in my room." The operator answered: "There are no black mice in the hotel—it must be a rat." A hotel employee with a flashlight arrived in time to see the rat run off into its hole. Shirley resumed writing her letter, adding a P.S.: "When you come here bring one of the large—not the small—traps from the cellar." Charles arrived in due course

Shirley never lost her taste for Cokes. *Credit: Baron Wolman for PEOPLE.*

Never having been to black Africa, Shirley was determined to know all she could before she left Woodside. *Baron Wolman for PEOPLE.*

with not one but two traps. That night they heard the right kind of snap, and Shirley threw the rat's body into the hotel corridor.

Shirley was like no other United Nations delegate had been before or since. For one thing, there was always a group of her fans in the visitors' galleries less interested in the course of international debate than in seeing a former movie star. She'd sometimes flash the V-sign at her younger admirers. For another thing, although she understood it, she didn't speak and write in the peculiarly obfuscating jargon of the international bureaucracy. She had a language of her own. "Yummy"—still—was one of her favorite

Ambassador Black discusses her political and diplomatic career with author Robert Windeler. *Baron Wolman for PEOPLE.*

A diplomat spends a lot of time on the telephone. *Baron Wolman for PEOPLE.*

words. She used colorful metaphors ("As my Holland ancestors have said, there are two flood tides beating up against the dikes") and phrases from contemporary pop-sociology: "social alienation," "criminal depravity," "colonial exploitation," "philosophical umbrellas."

A delegate from India asked the United States to clarify two technical points, one on national sovereignty and one on airborne sensing techniques pertaining to outer space. Shirley, as the senior U.S. representative present, replied: "Earlier this year I had the honor to serve on the Citizens' Group of the United Nations Task Force. We know that our planet is an earth spaceship, and all of us are on it together. My delegation feels that through the peaceful use of space we shall be able to achieve peace on our spaceship." The Indian delegate retorted: "After hearing the stirring appeal of the representative of the United States, I think I am more confused than ever."

"I always wrote my own speeches," Shirley recalled, "although I had to get them cleared at the U.S. Mission. I went a little too far when I talked about the refugee problem in the Middle East. I compared the problem there to the way America had treated the American Indians. The Indians were our first refugees. I expressed my feelings very colorfully, but the Mission felt it was

too harsh. They asked me to soften it, which I did."

Shirley never felt that her skimpy formal education was a detriment to her career at the United Nations or subsequently. Director John Ford had named her "One-Take Temple" because of her ability as a child to get things right the first time. And at the U.N. Charles W. Yost, the head of the U.S. delegation, assigned her to thirteen committees when the normal load was four because she was able to absorb reams of documents and keep up. Yost's basic advice to her: "Just be yourself." "I'm a fast learner and interested in a lot of things," she said. "We all grow. Hopefully one doesn't grow wider necessarily, but more in the brain department. I've had a unique opportunity my whole life to learn. I was studying Mandarin Chinese for six months at age eight, for a movie called *Stowaway*. I can still say a few key words, like 'very good'."

The Mainland Chinese hadn't yet arrived during Shirley's U.N. term, though she continued to push for their entry, but there were delegates from more than 100 countries ready to pronounce her performance in the thirteen-week General Assembly run "very good." "People were eager to discount her as a dilettante and featherbrain," said one U.N. expert, "but she proved them wrong. She took the job very seriously, did her homework and really worked—and before long was highly regarded by almost everybody there." Saudi Arabian Ambassador Jamil Baroody called Shirley "a fresh breeze that has gently blown in our midst." A fellow U.S. delegate noted that "Shirley is the only one of us who is always on time for appointments." And Mrs. Victoire Golengo of Congo (Brazzaville) found Shirley "a very pleasant person who takes everything very easily. Even when her government is criticized she doesn't get excited."

Unflappable and almost always smiling, Shirley was forty-one when she was at the U.N., plumpish and given to brightly-colored dresses, especially Puccis. Her hemlines—in the age of the mini-skirt—stayed below her chubby knees. She was paid at the rate of $38,000 a year, but only for the three months of the General Assembly session. She turned down a delegate from Morocco and a delegate from Greece who wanted to organize a showing of old Shirley Temple movies at the U.S. Mission or at the U.N. itself "because I thought my motives might be misunderstood."

U.N. Delegate Shirley Temple Black's typical day began at 6:30 A.M., the hour she had started getting up at the height of her movie career. Exercises to keep trim and help keep her weight down were done on the floor. "I know all the exercises. I've been doing them forever, I think." She cooked her own breakfast in the suite's small kitchen, met her bodyguard in the lobby and went by limousine to the U.S. Mission, arriving by 8:45 A.M. She attended committee meetings, ate official lunches and spent most evenings at diplomatic receptions. On rare nights off she cooked soup in the suite and studied her work for the next day. One of Charles's visits to Shirley in New York was for the weekend of the United Nations Ball at the Grand Ballroom of the Hotel Waldorf-Astoria where, like some younger version of Arthur and Kathryn Murray, they dipped and swooped through 1940s- and 1950s-style foxtrots and rhumbas.

At a dinner given by the Jordanian delegation Shirley choked on a pine nut (from a "yummy" rice dish) that had lodged in her throat. "I started to black out," she remembered. "But then I thought to myself, 'I'm a representative of the United States and I'm the only one here, and I can't die. If I do, nobody will believe that somebody didn't do something to me on purpose.' Finally the nut went down." Sitting across from the head of the Soviet Mission to the U.N., Yakov Malik, she then "presented to him what I call 'my jovial idea.' I suggested that there be only women on the Security Council." Malik never replied to the suggestion.

Shirley's committee assignments included refugees, social progress, the aging, and the peaceful uses of outer space, but her "two favorites" were the committees on youth and the environment, "which suddenly came together, because the youth of this country got extremely interested in environmental problems." Her maiden speech at the U.N. was the object of a barrage of critical letters because she had urged that the age of majority be lowered from twenty-one to eighteen, a theme left over from her 1967 campaign.

"I think we could stop a lot of protesting if eighteen-year-olds could do the same things adults do," she said. "They would feel more like participants in our society if they had the right to vote, paid taxes and were able to marry without parental consent. The youth of today are a very special generation. I admire them greatly. They're better educated and better informed, and when they protest, they're calling us, and I think we have to listen a little better."

In her official U.N. biographical sketch Shirley listed her profession as "former actress." She said, while acknowledging that her fame helped her get attention and get things done, "fame is fleeting, and it's very sad for people to wallow in the past. The happiest moment is now." She got along with delegates from "all countries except two which would not talk to me—Albania and Cuba—because I am American." In front of the U.S. Mission one day some Black Panthers were agitating. "I'm not afraid to extend my hand to anybody," she said, "although sometimes it hangs there for a long time. So I put my hand out and said, 'Hello, I'm Shirley Temple Black.' And the fellow said, 'Hello, I am a Black Panther.' And the very brutal-looking man got tears in his eyes and said, 'Oh, I remember.' "

When her U.N. term was up, just before Christmas 1969, Shirley was frustrated by all the work undone. "The term should be two years," she said. (Nixon, of course, could have appointed her again, but didn't.) Shirley had made a particular effort to understand and get to know the representatives of the developing nations of the unaligned Third World, and she was particularly popular with them. On the last day of the twenty-fourth U.N. General Assembly, one of her special friends, Angie Brooks from Liberia, was elected President of the General Assembly for the next session. While women from Third World countries often outnumbered the men and led delegations, Shirley had occupied the token U.S. "woman's seat" at the U.N. and showed no predisposition to broaden the role of her sex in international diplomacy.

In fact, at a Republican fund-raising dinner in Philadelphia in October 1970, Shirley denounced one human development of the day. "I don't care for Women's Lib—I prefer the strong arms of my husband around me," she said. She agreed that women had "the right to equal pay, equal opportunity and equal education, but argued that she was "not too fond of some of the methods which have been used to achieve those goals, like bra burning. I was liberated when I was three. I did get equal everything, certainly equal pay."

Shirley did acknowedge that she occasionally had been discriminated against at international gatherings where she was the only woman. "I have been asked to get coffee and sandwiches for the men. I did it at first, but I solved the problem by bringing my own coffee with me to work. So I had my coffee when the rest of the group convened and it wasn't that easy for them to send me out, and pretty soon they were bringing in things for everybody, like cookies. I solved the problem by being subtle because the best thing about being a woman is being feminine. That is where we can contribute so much, because we have a different viewpoint."

At a dinner party in an ambassador's home in another country she wouldn't name for fear of embarrassing it, Shirley had another problem. "I was the only woman at the dinner party and there were thirteen other countries there. After dinner, when the men went into the other room for brandy cigars, I didn't know what to do. I joined them for a few minutes, then asked the ambassador if his wife was there. She was upstairs, and I joined her there."

Despite her failure to be reappointed to the U.S. delegation to the U.N., Shirley left salaried U.N. work as she had entered it: a total believer in the organization. "We would have to invent the U.N. if we did not have it, which is not an original thought," she said. "The U.N. acts as the world's conscience, and over eighty-five percent of the work that is done by the United Nations is in the social, economic, educational and cultural fields. That doesn't make headlines like the Security Council does when someone is fighting. These good works are done by U.N. people aorund the world, but most of the funds and most of the energy are voluntarily contributed."

Shirley herself became a U.N. volunteer in 1970, visiting countries as varied as Iran, Rumania and Egypt to make speeches about pollution and endangered species. Later in the year she was appointed by Secretary of State William Rogers to be deputy chairman of the U.S. delegation to the Conference on Human Environment, which took place in Stockholm two years later. She was paid a per diem of $25 and found herself the only woman among 400 men at a preparatory meeting in Stockholm in 1971. That year she was also one of the few women invited to a Nixon White House dinner celebrating the twenty-fifth anniversary of the signing of the United Nations Charter, after the protests over the original plan to make it a stag affair. She used the occasion to ask the administration to submit the Indo-China War to the U.N. Security Council for settlement, although she had previously supported Nixon's handling of the war.

The two-week Stockholm Conference itself, in June 1972, was attended by business leaders and diplomats from 114 countries (only nine of them represented by any women, however) and was, in Shirley's words "the most successful world meeting that was ever held—so meaningful that it will be four or five years until the world is really aware of it. We took action on 109 different topics (including endangered species of fur-bearing animals) and drew up a declaration of the human environment, providing guidelines to improving the quality of human existence and insuring human dignity. It has to be an international solution because the air just sweeps around the world without a passport, not respecting boundaries, in about ten days, dropping pollution everywhere. Ocean and river pollution are also international."

Shirley's speech to the final session of the conference—written with only an hour and a half's notice—urging "the acknowledgment of our kinship as human beings and working together for the rational management of our common resources" won very good notices. It was printed in a paper that came out of the conference and widely reprinted around the world, along with the texts of speeches by Indira Gandhi, Barbara Ward and Margaret Mead.

As an international celebrity Shirley got to meet Yugoslavia's President Tito in Brioni, Yugoslavia; and a Malaysian merchant told her "you were my first crush" in a Moscow restaurant, during her work with the American-Soviet Joint Committee in the Field of Environmental Protection. She addressed members of the same group in Washington on the subject of whales, the largest endangered species of mammals, trying to persuade the Russians to give up whaling as the U.S. had already done. Appropriately in San Francisco ("my home is on the San Andreas Fault"), Shirley announced on behalf of the U.N. to 170 earthquake experts that a worldwide natural disaster "early warning system" was in the planning stages. The system, designed to provide warning against earthquakes, volcanic eruptions, floods, tidal waves and typhoons, would require every country on earth to participate.

Back in Washington, Shirley made a movie for the first time in twenty-four years. She narrated a twenty-minute film about a barber of Honduras who became one of the Western Hemisphere's most admired primitive painters, Jose Antonio Velasquez, for the Visual Aids Division of the Organization of American States in the Pan American Union. It was one of a series of OAS films for which film stars provided the voice-over narration without appearing on camera. Shirley was selected for Velasquez because his story was presented "like a tale for children." Her travels to many parts of the globe got her into "the darndest situations sometimes because on TV and in some movie houses around the world I'm still a little girl. It confuses people, I suppose."

It was little wonder, then, that she found her next full-time assignment somewhat less appealing. In late 1972 Shirley was appointed to the President's Council on Environmental Quality (CEQ), where she seemed to specialize in "sewage and sludge" in her homeland. A typical field trip in that post was a five-hour canoe ride through Four Holes Swamp, a black-water sanctuary in South Carolina with virgin cypress and "very good water, full of nutrients. Also full of alligators, cottonmouths." She resigned quietly from CEQ in January 1974 to plot a return to international affairs.

One reason that Shirley felt comfortable about volunteering for work that took her traveling, and so often abroad, was that her three children had grown up without causing major problems for their parents or themselves. Susan, Charles Jr. and Lori all might be a little square and dull by many of their contemporaries' standards, but at least they weren't hooked on drugs or alcohol like some other parents' offspring. Nor were they talentless chips trying to launch careers off the old show business block, like other children of Hollywood. "Except for minor traffic offenses," said Shirley, "we've had no trouble."

Susan graduated from Stanford University with a degree in art history, painted for pleasure and wrote a play and several drafts of a novel. Charles earned an undergraduate degree in political science and planned a career in international affairs. Lori, in her mother's words "plays the piano very well, is also good with animals—has even gotten into the tank with killer whales, and has always majored in boys." She studied music through college.

The three had extremely conventional and con-

She's long since switched from checkers to chess, which she attempts to explain to the author in her Woodside living room. *Baron Wolman for PEOPLE.*

93

servative Northern California social lives, more in the tradition of the Blacks than of the Temples. All of them, even while in school and during their wide travels, considered themselves as living at home, either in the Tudor house in Woodside or in the rich dark-wooded ambassador's residence in Accra, Ghana, and Charles Jr.'s longish hair and mustache were as much rebellion as they ever evidenced. "I raised them pretty much as I was raised," Shirley explained. "We have wide open communication—that is very important. No matter what they tell you, you must not be visibly shocked. And you must teach them that they need a sense of humor to survive."

In Woodside the Blacks held a "family council every night," rotating the leadership of the discussion. "We discuss *everything*," Shirley said, "politics, what they are doing, what Charles and I are doing. After about age sixteen it is their own direction that they go in, however. Children are sort of on loan to you, you have the pleasure of having them. You don't have that long a time to make your point with your childrn, and when they are older there is not much more you can give them, except to be available and to keep the door open."

One thing about which Shirley almost never wanted to talk, with the children or anyone else, was finances. "I just don't feel it's very feminine to talk about money," she explained, although she did not feel it was unfeminine to make it. "I don't think it's good taste to talk about it, either." Shirley was a fiscal conservative at home as well as in her politics ("let's say I'm careful"), which came from "having a banker for a father" and growing up in those Depression years. My earnings have been greatly exaggerated by the press, although I can assure you that I will never be hungry or poor or not able to take care of my share of the children's future."

Two matters relating to finances that really galled Shirley were: 1) the fact that she worked on straight salary for the studios (albeit high salaries for the times) and therefore had no financial participation in re-releases of her films, to television or otherwise; and 2) the accusation that she had bought political position and prominence. "The truth of the matter," she said in late 1974, "is that Charles and I have contributed exactly $1,167 to the Republican party in the last four years—and only $307 of that went to national campaigns. There's no political payoff." (Not for

money, at least, but her volunteer time and efforts on behalf of her party were certainly partly rewarded by her appointments to government posts.)

Beyond those particular items, "money is not of great interest to me," she insisted. "Oh, I like to see things turn out successfully. That is the creative part of business. I'm interested to see that something I'm involved with doesn't fail. But my money is managed by a bank's trust officers, although I like to be knowledgable about what is going on with it. I don't like to be left out of those decisions."

In the spring of 1975 the Independent Broadcasting Authority, which regulates Britain's independent television network (ITV), decided that Shirley Temple movies "have no relevance to modern children" and would not be shown during the network's "children's hour." "We felt they were just too sentimental and mawkish to interest today's sophisticated children," said a spokesman for the Authority. "It was felt that Shirley Temple singing 'On the Good Ship Lollipop' or 'Animal Crackers in My Soup' had no relevance today. Her films are more likely to appeal to the nostalgia of older people."

Shirley herself had long since arrived at more or less the same conclusion. "We have twenty-two prints of my old films out back in the toolshed in Woodside," she said. "Sometimes my son used to dust them off and show them to his friends. At first I thought they regarded them as high camp, but they really seemed to enjoy them." She never watched her movies in their frequent television reruns. In fact, her only viewing of anyone's motion pictures in the 1960s and 1970s was "on airplanes, and I'm not sure I'm a good judge. I fell asleep during *The Sting* and it won an Academy Award. I also fell asleep when I saw *The French Connection* on a plane. And that won the Academy Award. Maybe when I fall asleep in a movie it's a good sign."

In 1972 Shirley put away the last of her childish things; with her own daughters fully grown, she gave her doll collection to the Stanford Children's Hospital, where at any given time about 500 of her dolls are on display in the reception area. She kept several Shirley Temple mugs, cereal bowls and cream pitchers but proceeded to wash them in the dishwater to get her image off them; "I love blue glass but I'm awfully tired of that face," she explained. And she no longer had Hollywood friends. "I knew a lot of people there when I was a child," she said, "but most of them have gone to the Great Beyond. I was so young I wasn't really close to that many people, anyway."

At age fifty in 1978, Shirley's dimpled cheeks and dark flashing eyes were the same as they had been in movies. But the blonde curls were a long distant memory, and her very dark hair was swept back in an almost matronly do. Her figure was plumpish but well-rounded on her five-foot-two frame. Uncannily, her laugh, actually part giggle, went straight back at least to *Stand Up and Cheer* in 1934, although coming from an adult mouth it sometimes seemed more nervous than spontaneous.

Living down her former self, she said, was "not a problem within my circle of friends or really with anyone except a few older people who are stuck on this image of the little girl. That's their problem." When she traveled, many people recognized her right away, and her name always opened doors—"some have told me it's like having a distant relative visit, someone they've known all their lives." But when she posed for a photograph with the President of the United Nations General Assembly in 1974, he said, "Thank you very much, Miss MacLaine." And that wasn't the only time she had been taken for the tall, red-haired Shirley MacLaine.

"For years I tried to get into Red China," said Shirley Black, still using Cold War terminology in the mid-1970's. "I didn't think I'd have a hard time because I was one of three Americans who signed a petition asking for China's admission to the United Nations and sent it to President Nixon. When I mentioned it to Henry Kissinger, he said, 'Shhh, don't talk about it.' I didn't know he was already preparing for China's admission. An answer to my application to get into Red China never came, but Shirley MacLaine got a letter inviting *her* to come to China. I'm sure the letter was meant for me; they got their Shirleys confused."

One of the lessons she learned in her forties, Shirley noted, was "never to give a definite answer—yes or no—anymore. I used to give very definite answers when I was about fifteen. At sixteen one is the oldest one ever is in life. You think you know everything. People would ask, 'Are you going to do such and such?' and I'd say, 'Oh, no, I'd never do that'—very definite and very likely untrue. So I'm very careful of that now,

because I don't know where life is taking me, where any road will lead. I'd never have dreamed of working at the United Nations, which didn't even exist when I was a child, or of being an ambassador."

Her various jobs, she claimed, just happened along. "I don't go looking for work. I seem to be a born volunteer and I've always been interested in people and projects. Maybe I should have been a reporter. When there is a need and I can do something about it, I am happy to do it. I am also happy to say that I've made no enemies that I know of. The only people who wouldn't talk to me are the Albanians; but then, they won't talk to anyone else either."

Shirley felt that everything that had happened in her life was useful and had somehow prepared her for international relations. The cast of characters had changed from the likes of Mussolini's sons and Eleanor Roosevelt, to Golda Meir and Anwar Sadat. ("She's the most fascinating woman in the world and he is the man with the most charisma," said Shirley of the latter two. "Now that's spoken like a true diplomat, isn't it?") But along the way she had learned to shop. ("I buy quality, not quantity, because it lasts longer and is more frugal. I'm not much on high fashion; I simply can't be frivolous because I travel so much, I like to wear serious clothes.") She had learned to fly from continent to continent with only two suitcases, but always with room left over for her emergency chocolate rations. And she learned how to write her own speeches, how to get all her homework done and how to keep from drinking too much at embassy functions.

In her own home Shirley indulged in cooking and gardening, and the garden in Woodside contained, in addition to immensely practical crops such as lettuce, potatoes and tomatoes, tiny Tahitian gardenias ("my favorite flower") and trees bearing Meyer lemons ("they are so sweet you don't need sugar to make lemonade"). Although she had been working with the Sierra Club and the National Wildlife Federation and was, along with Charles and their children, interested in conservation and the environment, she noted that "it wasn't until Earth Day, 1970, that I really felt the environmental movement was going to play a dominant place in my life—and in that of my family."

From that point, apart from her formal work on the national and international level, Shirley's chil-

95

dren recycled cans and newspapers. Lori worked at Sealife Park, with sea lions, porpoises, killer whales and various fish, and spent six weeks at an Outward Bound program in the Sierra Mountains, where one project was to live alone for thirty-six hours, finding water and wild food to live on. Charles Jr. was an ardent backpacker, and Susan's special outdoor love was riding horses. All of them went away to camp, a working ranch in Arizona where they raised their own animals and vegetables.

"Being all native Californians, we are naturally outdoor people," Shirley said. "We have a reverence for nature and we feel very strongly that people must learn to live with nature and not try to conquer it. In the past we've taken everything for granted—the fruits of the soil and so on—and now we can't take *anything* for granted. The world has awakened to the environmental problem, to the mess that we find ourselves in, and it's now a question of how we are going to live our lives, how we use our own personal energies and our natural resources that we know have limits. It can't be talk anymore, but it must be a new living ethic that affects every citizen."

Shirley, as a tomboy in Santa Monica, had learned to fish, and she and Charles still loved to fish together, especially for steelheads in northern California and the Pacific Northwest, on trips lasting as long as five days. "And we eat all we catch," she said. Charles, as President of Mardela International, worked in aquaculture among such groups as the Lummi and Paiute Indians in North America, and with the government of Yugoslavia.

Charles taught countries to catch more and better fish and to set up cold storage places for fish. He taught the Lummis to raise Belgian oysters and to "grow" strong domestic trout. In a two-year project with Yugoslavia, Charles provided "good strong American catfish for matrimony with Yugoslavian catfish," as Shirley delicately put it. "Charlie designed the shipping boxes and sent some 180,000 catfish over to Yugoslavia, where catfish are considered to be quite a delicacy and sell for the equivalent of $1.50 a pound. His main love has always been the ocean and fish and he has this unique ability to combine business with fish. He is a Pisces. I'm a Taurus, a worrier. Taurus people find out quickly who they can trust." She felt that the real strength of their relationship was that "my husband and I are both on our own courses, but they're complementary. You can't

just have love, which is the most important thing, you must also have interests that are somewhat the same."

Shirley considered that most of her life had "been free from stumbling blocks," and never liked to dwell on problems, her own or anyone else's—"I want to know what's going to happen tomorrow," she was fond of saying. But what happened to Shirley Temple Black in the autumn of 1972 was a problem that had to be dealt with immediately and head on: cancer of the breast. The American Cancer Society said it was a problem for seven out of every one hundred women, and Shirley, after thinking, "Oh God, why is this happening to me?" decided to share the experience of her mastectomy publicly. She became the first well-known woman to do so, two years before Betty Ford and Happy Rockefeller. "Maybe that was the reason it happened to me," she said, "so I could tell the women of the world, who are my sisters, that they should go to the doctor for diagnosis when they have unusual symptoms, and that they should learn to examine themselves."

She discovered the lump on her left breast herself, in September 1972 in Washington D.C. "right after I had taken a bath. As soon as I got home to California I called my doctor and he gave me a mammography, which is an X-ray of the breast, and decided I should have a biopsy to see whether the tumor was benign or malignant. He said my chances were about 60/40, which I thought were pretty good odds." Between Shirley's schedule and the doctor's it was November 1 before she entered the hospital and November 2 before the biopsy was performed.

"I wouldn't let them go any further," she said. "I only signed the release to let them do the biopsy. I said, 'Doctor, you make the incision, and I'll make the decision.' Because it's my body. I have the right to decide what happens to that body. I think if the cancer had metastasized, spread all over my body, maybe I would choose not to have any surgery at all." This was unusual, since if the tumor turned out to be malignant, doctors preferred to perform the mastectomy right away rather than put the patient through two separate anesthetics and operations. But Shirley recalled a girlfriend of hers who went to the hospital, didn't pay too much attention to what she was signing and woke up without a breast.

Nevertheless, when Shirley woke up from her biopsy, the doctor, with Charles's help, told her

In the brief weeks between her appointment to the ambassadorial post and her arrival in Ghana, Shirley had little time for sitting with her setter Ringo in the backyard at Woodside. *Photo by Ellen Graham.*

that the tumor was removed but that it had been malignant and a mastectomy would have to be performed. "After I fully recovered from the anesthetic I had a good cry over the whole thing," Shirley recalled, "and my daughters came to the hospital and we all cried for a while. When that was over I decided that we would go ahead with the operation, a modified radical mastectomy, which is the removal of the breast and some lymph nodes in the armpit—twelve nodes out of about eighty in the armpit."

The tumor itself had been only two centimeters in length, and the malignant part was no bigger than the tip of Shirley's fingernail. "The decision to have the operation wasn't too difficult to make," said Shirley, "since the alternative was to die. The operation is an ugly operation, and it is a maiming operation, and it takes a while to get used to your revised body, so I don't want to be too light about the subject or mislead anyone." Still, with characteristic dedication, Shirley did a Dinah Shore TV talk show just two days before the operation—"we both put on seven pounds that day, eating Russian food until it came out of our ears," Dinah recalled, and three days after the operation Shirley announced it to the world. Within a month she was back at work with the Council of Environmental Quality.

"The first time I came out of the anesthetic I said, 'seabed,' " Shirley remembered, "and Charlie said, 'you're still at that meeting in Geneva.' I went back to sleep, and the second time I came to I said, 'chocolate.' Now that's the real me. Susan was sitting by my bed and she went out and bought me some of those little chocolate kisses. There is probably quite a bit of depression after any operation because of the anesthetic and the shock to your system. What I did was cry when I felt like crying, even in front of the children. Some people suggest that you should go cry alone so that you don't depress your family but I think you have to be yourself: when you feel unhappy, let everybody know it so long as you don't carry it to the extreme."

Shirley's room in the hospital "looked like a gangster's funeral," and within a few hours she was walking around the halls like Lady Bountiful, dispensing floral tributes to those patients who had fewer than she. Reporters and admirers, dressed up as nurses and attendants, tried to sneak into her room, but Lori and Susan took turns standing guard during the day and Charles rolled a cot into the room to stay with Shirley at night. During the two days after the operation Shirley discussed with the three of them the possibility of making the mastectomy public "to get the word 'cancer' and the removal of a breast talked about." Charles Jr. was on a fishing boat off Panama but fortunately called in and agreed with the others that Mom should speak out.

Accordingly, Shirley went on radio and television and wrote an article on the whole experience in the February, 1973 McCall's, which elicited more than fifty thousand letters from people who had had or were contemplating mastectomies—including three men. "I don't think there's anything worse than talking about your operation," she said. "But I did want to urge all women to have checkups and to check themselves, because the whole thing came as quite a surprise to me, a very unpleasant shock. I got one very interesting letter from a woman in Oakland who said she had been slightly offended to see that I was describing in a magazine how I had my breast removed, but that same evening while she was showering she had found a lump in her own breast. She was writing from the hospital having just had a mastectomy, and she was grateful. That alone made my writing about it worthwhile."

There were adjustments to be made. ("As soon as I learned how to pronounce 'prosthesis' I went out and bought one.") Three weeks after surgery Shirley made a speech on the environment, in Chicago, that she had committed herself to six months previously. "I had three silk scarves to wear, all sentimental," she recalled. "One I had worn when I met President Roosevelt, and during my speech one of my scarves came out. I felt like Sally Rand."

While it usually takes five years to be sure the cancer won't recur, Shirley was pronounced cured and assured she could resume a full work schedule. "I'm grateful to God, my family and the doctors," she said at the time, "because I have much more to accomplish before I'm through." Charles, she noted later, hadn't "changed since the operation. Our love is very strong. We looked at the problem without shame and directly, and well, he's just my life. We're going along as normal. I don't think that people should think about changing after an operation of this sort. I think if you had a good husband before, he'll be a good husband. If you had a rotten husband before, I really don't think he's going to change. And if you have a good marriage, nothing is really going to hurt it."

In the late spring and early summer of 1974 Shirley was, by her own reckoning, "a woman of leisure." In May she became the first woman to be appointed to the board of directors of Walt Disney Productions ("window dressing," a Disney executive conceded). And that, despite her ongoing membership in the Screen Actors' Guild, was as much involvement with the film industry as she ever wanted again. "I have been a union member for forty-three years," she noted, "and now I think it's time they gave me a testimonial dinner and a gold watch."

The name Shirley Temple Black, and the person, now appeared as a director on the boards of Disney, Del Monte (Foods) Corporation, the United States Association for the United Nations, the National Wildlife Federation and the National Multiple Sclerosis Society. In addition, Shirley was doing volunteer work with the U.N.'s Food and Agriculture Organization, and was a member of the U.S. Commission for UNESCO. But as she put it, succinctly and typically, since her resignation from the President's Council on Environmental Quality in January, she had been "keeping busy but with no salary coming in." She wanted and

Shirley Temple Black and Jane Withers reminisce with varying degrees of enthusiasm, Hollywood, December 1976. *Photograph by Peter C. Borsari.*

didn't know of her childhood film career, but did know of her work at the U.N. A leading Ghanaian intellectual visiting the United States at the time of Shirley's appointment said his countrymen and women would be open-minded and that her most important potential qualification would be her influence in Washington. "As a woman and a former movie star maybe people in the United States will listen to what she has to say about us," he said. "What's important is that she be well disposed toward Africa and capable of providing reasonable and sensible advice to her own country."

A high official at the State Department had told her just before she was publicly named as ambassador to expect some adverse reaction in the United States. "We know what you can do and the other countries know what you can do but most American journalists and the general public aren't aware that you're capable," he said. "I know me," Shirley added at the time. "I know how I feel and I feel a kinship with all human beings. It's just that I can't say I feel capable because I don't want to have that quoted before the Senate hearings."

Awaiting the U.S. Senate hearings on her confirmation, Shirley spent her time "mostly reading and thinking" about this latest role she'd been offered, and about the little country more than 7,500 miles from Woodside that she hadn't yet seen. She recalled Eleanor Roosevelt: "I see a link between Mrs. Roosevelt's later years and my own recent activities," Shirley said. "A lot of her work in international affairs has got to me by osmosis and been an inspiration to me at the United Nations and in the five years since," she added.

That might seem like heresy for the lifelong "Republican but independent" whose devotion to her political party had ranged from stuffing envelopes and walking precincts to running for Congress and giving speeches for free, and had resulted in a string of what were essentially, after all, political appointments. But Shirley had an image problem from this second public career as well as from her first, in films. In her first and last try for elective office, that 1967 special primary election for the U.S. House of Representatives, she had been unfairly lumped with Ronald Reagan and George Murphy in the right-wing ex-actor school of California politics. "Really I'm a fiscal conservative, liberal to moderate on domestic issues, and very liberal internationally," she

stated. "People don't realize what I've been doing all these years," she complained. "Even now when I'm at home, some friends still think I'm at the U.N."

The U.S. Senate, perhaps sensing that Shirley's people-to-people ambassadorship might be more effective at that time in the history of the United States and Ghana than one based on a sounder intellectual record, and certainly weary of the Watergate mess and the consequent mass distrust of professional politicians, swiftly—and unanimously—confirmed Shirley Temple Black as U.S. envoy to Ghana. Her confirmation on September 12, 1974, and those of former Kentucky Senator John Sherman Cooper as the first U.S. Ambassador to East Germany, and of former presidential economic advisor Kenneth Rush as Ambassador to France, gave the Ford administration its first three diplomatic appointments.

In the next two-and-a-half months Shirley had fifty-five official State Department briefings on Ghana and United States diplomacy, "and Lord knows how many unofficial ones," she recalled. "The State Department made me feel as though I'd already served in Ghana and was ready for a new assignment. But at least I felt confident when I got to Accra." She also talked with professors of economics, political science and sociology, and businessmen whose firms had large investments in Ghana. She took a crash brush-up course in French and read books and documents in her most conscientious "one-take Temple" style. Shirley, Charles and Susan (who were to accompany her to Ghana, leaving Charles Jr. and Lori at home to finish college) each had several vaccinations against exotic African diseases.

On November 29, 1974, Shirley took a wistful look around the Woodside house and drove with the family up to the San Francisco airport, where she left behind the life of a California suburban matron for her posting in sweltering sub-Saharan Africa. Although Shirley's predecessor in Accra, Fred L. Hadsell, had held his job for three years, and she might be in Ghana even longer, it never occurred to her and Charles to sell the Woodside house. Shirley's parting shot to Charles Jr. was "don't take off the mustache, I'm gettin' to like it." And to newsmen who followed her to the airplane she confided that she had turned down several European diplomatic posts—not necessarily at the ambassadorial level—and a job as an agency head in Washington, in order to go exactly where she was headed today. "If I could have picked a place to serve it would have been in black Africa," she asserted.

The Ghana she arrived in was suffering from rampant inflation worsened by quadrupled world oil prices; a shortage of investment capital from abroad; and a stagnant agriculture. None of these was visible as Shirley, Charles and Susan stepped off the plane in Accra, and all was temporarily forgotten in the warmth of welcome in English—or "Awwaaba" in the Twi tribal language. Men in the tropical worsted suits that are one of the legacies of British colonialism and men and women in garments of colorful local cotton cloth waved and shouted to Madam Ambassador and her family. Ghana, once a prime shipping point for slaves going to America, was considered one of the friendliest nations in Africa. Although its government was a military dictatorship, there was a minimum of bureaucracy and there were few overt trappings of a police state. Its Twi, Ga and Shanti tribes were open, hospitable and confident.

As a successful career woman, Ambassador Black had been ideally selected for Ghana, where women's liberation slogans were found even in the most remote villages. And, as a long-term and outspoken opponent of racial separation in a country vocally and vigorously involved in supporting African liberation movements all over the continent, Shirley was championed by both Ghana's men and women from the instant of her arrival. She quickly became one of Ghana's "wanto wazuri," which in Ashanti means "beautiful people."

Four days after her arrival Shirley presented her credentials to the Ghanaian head of state, Colonel Ignatius Acheampong, leader of the country's ruling military junta, in the stately sort of princess-comes-to-the-palace ceremony she had loved since childhood. In fact, the presentation of credentials ceremony was worthy both of the former Gold Coast's British background and Shirley's Hollywood one. "It was probably the most thrilling moment of my life," she said. "Standing alone in a little canopied setting with the Ghanaian Air Force band playing 'The Star Spangled Banner' was almost too much. I was covered in gooseflesh. Then the talking drums of welcome really covered me with gooseflesh; the talking drums go all the way to the pit of your stomach. To me it was like the pages of *The National Geographic* magazine come to life."

She stepped forward from her canopy and presented a leather portfolio from Washington to Colonel Acheampong, and in a strong clear voice with the tight accent of her native California she said: "Your excellency, I am deeply honored to present the letters by which the President of the United States Gerald R. Ford accredits me as ambassador extraordinary and plenipotentiary of the United States of America to the Republic of Ghana. Thank you." And Shirley Temple Black was now "Her Excellency" and ready to go to work.

Acheampong impressed her as a "serious, hard-working and determined man of vision." Shirley visited Kumasi in Ghana's central region and called on the country's most important tribal chief, Otumfuo Opoku II, the Asantehen of the Ashanti tribe. Her first stop at a rural outhouse didn't faze her, since it was no worse than those on many movie locations. "The first one of these I was ever in, I was three years old," she noted. "Problems of this nature are never problems to rugged Californians." She further suggested that one of the six cubicles have her name on it: "one for the ambassador."

The ambassador's residence she shared with Charles and Susan in Accra was comfortable and well staffed without being the country club that many embassies are, even in developing nations. "Charlie's on the road a lot," she explained several months into her residency, "advising many countries how to improve their commercial fishing resources. But he can't work in Ghana since I'm the ambassador and that might pose a conflict of interest. He gets back here often enough for us to have a good home life. Susan roams around the country, visiting villages and attending durbars (official receptions). She's already had her first article accepted by the Burlingame paper back in California, so she's a bona fide foreign correspondent now," beamed a proud mother.

Shirley's own trips to villages in the interior of Ghana from Accra on the coast were frequent, happy and noisy, as dozens of villagers greeted her at every stop. She flashed the dimples and smile, suggested to one expectant mother that she name a daughter—should she have one—Shirley, and tried to meet as many Ghanaians as she could, greeting each in a few words of his or her tribal language as well as in English, the country's official tongue. The shots she and the American members of her household had taken back

103

home successfully immunized them from disease, although they continued to take anti-malaria pills once a week. "In Ghana we have a variety of malaria that is quickly fatal," she explained, "and we must remember our every-Sunday ritual: malaria tablets with breakfast."

Shirley won more raves from Ghanaians—few of whom were concerned with her prior lives—than she had ever won from critics during her first career. She astonished the professional diplomats in her embassy by appearing for work in brightly-painted cotton gowns (often of orange, green and brown) with matching head scarves, of the sort favored by local women, and in earrings and bracelets of Ghanaian gold. With her gift for mimicry and languages she took to using native phrases such as the welcoming "awwaaabe" and "oyiwala donn" ("thank you" in Ga) in both official and informal conversation. She acquired a boxer puppy and dubbed him "ma danfo" ("my friend" in Twi).

Occasionally Shirley was mistaken for an actual American black, thanks to her California-based suntan, burnished and deepened by the West African sun, and her dark hair and eyes. And the ambassador was glad that her child star days were only dimly known in Ghana and that somebody somewhere had missed her movies. She was plainly tired of the foreign press in Ghana calling her a "former child star." "Dr. Kissinger was a former child, Jerry Ford was a former child, even FDR was a former child," she snapped, the dimples flashing to soften the pique. "I retired from the movies in 1949, but I'm still a former child." She laughed at her own anger and said more seriously, "I'm delighted at last to be thought of as a diplomat rather than as a film entertainer."

Still the movie pro's instincts were intact. On a visit to the Accra Polytechnic School, which was heavily photographed by television news teams, Shirley stepped from her limousine, tripped and stumbled—the cameras whirring the whole time. Her dancer's reflexes kept her from hitting the ground, but the newsmen stood silent. The nervous giggle erupted from Shirley and, in a smiling gesture reminiscent of that little girl who used to hold up her hand to spoil what she knew was a bad take, she said, "Wow, I blew it. Let's do that one over, boys." And the lady ambassador walked through another take, just as the little girl would have done.

Shirley's greatest triumph of ambassadorial choreography was with Accra's Market Women's Association, which runs nine percent of the country's stalls and shops and most of its fishing boats. These "market mammies," who tend toward physical hugeness to symbolize their vast commercial wealth and power, invited Shirley to visit the colorful outdoor Macoola market, where she embraced them as sister working girls.

"It was an exciting and heartwarming experience," she recalled. "They were all wearing local cloth and singing songs of welcome; they spread cloth on the ground in front of me. I didn't want to step on it until they explained it was a sign of welcome. So I stood on the cloth and did a High-life in my walking shoes." She spoke of the wriggling national dance as "not hard to learn. The music is complicated but the step itself is easy. The women seemed pleased that the United States has a lady ambassador here," she noted. "They like a woman with political strength."

Although she noted that "there are no major problems in U.S.–Ghana relations and the feelings are good," there were problems in Ghana that engaged her concern: the country's unsuccessful quest for its own oil in view of world oil prices, worldwide inflation and debts left over from the regime of Kwame Nkrumah. One hopeful note was the success of the government's "operation feed yourself" program to reduce dependence on imports. "My job is to stimulate American action here," she said, "and to look after the interests of my country in trade and diplomacy in Ghana. I'd like to see more done in terms of health assistance, particularly maternal child care, and in trying to encourage U.S. business interests to get involved."

At first she worked the embassy staff very hard, easing up a little after the first three months and then insisting only on fortnightly meetings instead of the weekly ones she had held at first. One of her subordinates termed her "easy to work with, very understanding, a thorough professional." "I work a seventeen-hour day, and I'm personally responsible for 108 staff members in the embassy," she said. "If anything goes wrong, I'm to blame. And if there are sudden developments, I'd have to make split-second decisions and they'd have to be the right ones. It's a tremendous work load but I have no regrets. I've not been bored for an instant. My biggest problem is that I rise at 6 A.M. and work steadily all day. At night there is almost always an official function that I must attend. And in Ghana everyone eats late; dinner seldom starts before 9 P.M. I get very little sleep but I still feel so robust I sometimes wear everybody else out."

In the fall of 1975, Madame Ambassador Black's daughter Susan was married to an official of the Italian embassy in Ghana, which reminded the world that Shirley Temple could become a grandmother—and caused a brief revival in Rome of Shirley Temple dolls, dresses and hairdos, and of the song "On the Good Ship Lollipop" in Italian. Susan's groom, Roberto Falaschi, besides being first secretary in his country's embassy in Accra, was the son of the Italian ambassador to Uganda. The couple had met within a month of Shirley's and Susan's arrival in Accra and were married at the U.S. embassy.

The new mother-in-law, a continued and outspoken advocate of black self-determination in Africa, was made an honorary deputy chief of the Fanti tribe. Wearing solid gold bangles on her chubby arms and a scarf and elegantly simple dress in muted gold colors, she was carried before a cheering throng of 20,000. "Four of them picked me up like a side of beef," she recalled. "Then they gave me my royal scepter and stool" (throne). Beyond such ceremonial participation in the life of Ghana, Shirley was able to devote much of her time to humanitarian—rather than political—concerns, particularly health and nutrition. The government in Ghana was stable during Shirley's tenure, and its relations with the U.S. were untroubled. She ensured that American government assistance programs to Ghana ran smoothly, taking particular interest in the provision of anti-measles vaccines and other health aids.

After less than two years in Africa, in July 1976, Shirley was appointed U.S. Chief of Protocol by President Ford on the advice of Secretary of State Kissinger. "I'm a great fan of hers—and it's not because of the movies," said Kissinger in praise of Shirley's "able and tough" handling of the Ghana post. "I'm pleased to be the first woman in 200 years to hold this job," she said. "I'm energetic, I'll work hard and I look forward to shaking up anything I see that needs shaking up."

She was sworn in at the White House, and couldn't resist wondering—despite her own anti-liberationist leanings—"why, Mr. President, it took 200 years for one of us to get the job." She carried the rank of Assistant Secretary of State and

commanded a staff of forty-four. She attended "every national day every country has—there are 126 of those a year," she said. Shirley also escorted visiting heads of state around Washington. She and Charles sublet a small apartment on the District's Massachusetts Avenue, where she did the cleaning and cooked dinner, and where Charles was able to spend sixty percent of his time. Shirley usually had lunch at the State Department cafeteria—and usually had "cottage cheese—the only thing I really missed in Ghana."

Her term was short-lived, however, as Ford was defeated in November. She widely announced her willingness to stay on as Protocol Chief under President Carter, but her Republicanism had been just too long-standing and partisan for that possibility. She attended Carter's inaugural gala January 19, 1977 at the Kennedy Center still with her old title, however, and was the last lame duck from the Ford administration, lasting three more days. At the gala she'd already lost her sense of humor; in the middle she asked, "When do we eat? I'm hungry."

In 1977, unemployed again, Shirley took a trip, as "private citizen," to Mainland China. Back in San Francisco she told the Commonwealth Club of California in a speech: "China's desire for friendship with the U.S. was a standard theme in every one of our official conversations—yet a very different song came from the clusters of loudspeakers mounted on poles out in the rice paddies, on train radios whose volume could not be reduced, and at the factory bench." She termed it a "drum fire of bitter invective" and said a pervasive theme was "the United States and all imperialists are paper tigers."

Terming the Chinese people themselves "unabashedly friendly and curious," she praised the fact that she saw "nobody loafing." She told the press before her address that Chinese leaders still had "high regard and respect" for Nixon. But asked if she thought the ex-President should return to public life, she snapped: "I think we've already had everything he has to give on the subject."

Ambassador Black, as she preferred to be called, turned aside a hopefully joking request from the Commonwealth Club's emcee to sing a verse of "On the Good Ship Lollipop." "Nothing could be sadder than a forty-nine-year-old woman singing a child's song," she replied. "I don't even do that at home."

Later in 1977, and back at the 20th Century-Fox lot, Shirley did appear to receive the Life Achievement Award of the American Center of Films for Children. Former co-star Darryl Hickman (*Kiss and Tell, A Kiss for Corliss*) praised her adult work as a diplomat: "Shirley has proved that a child actor can be something besides having dimples and being able to cry on cue." Jane Withers, Buddy Ebsen, Robert Young and Jack Oakie also spoke in praise of their former co-star.

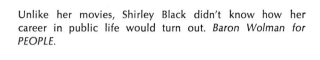

Unlike her movies, Shirley Black didn't know how her career in public life would turn out. *Baron Wolman for PEOPLE.*

Shirley's award was a bright red woman's shoe, the Ruby Slipper, named for the slipper worn by Dorothy in *The Wizard of Oz.* In accepting, Shirley said, "I had a perfect childhood. I'm not a sentimental person. The most important moment is now."

Nearing fifty, and looking around for another job in international diplomacy, Shirley Temple Black thought that "everything I've done in my life has directed me to this kind of career. Little Shirley opened a lot of doors for me, but if you don't have something to contribute, the doors can close very rapidly. We all learn a lot from the past —it's just that we shouldn't live there. I don't want to sit in a lovely house and look at old scrapbooks. I like to work. But I'll never make another movie, those days are over. I loved my life as a child. But this I find much harder work. There's no ending to the stories; it's not like having a script where it all works out neatly."

THE FILMS

Thugs about to kidnap "Diaper Dampsy's" grinning girlfriend in *Kid's Last Fight*.

THE SHORTS AND
THE BIT PARTS

1932

Educational Films, to which Shirley was signed in January 1932, at age three, for ten dollars a day, had been founded in 1919 to make short films for schools. But that notion had failed, and Educational had turned to cheapjack comedy shorts. The Baby Burlesks ("the best things I ever did," said Shirley as an adult) were one-reelers featuring small children—no taller than three feet—satirizing adults, and adult movies. They were vaguely exploitative, racist and not necessarily intended for children. The kids all wore diapers with enormous safety pins, with adult costumes on the upper halves of their bodies. The Baby Burlesks took an average of four days to shoot. Shirley appeared in eight of them, four in 1932, and four in 1933.

The first was *War Babies*, a send-up of the World War I movie *What Price Glory?* Shirley played Dolores Del Rio playing Charmaine. Her first screen words were "Mais oui, mon cher," spoken to a diapered soldier boy; she didn't understand them. In *The Runt Page*, a spoof of *The Front Page*, she played Lulu Parsnips (columnist Louella Parsons, who later became one of Shirley's greatest champions). In *Pie Covered Wagon*, a takeoff on *Covered Wagon*, she was tied to a stake while baby Indians threw dirt at her. In *Glad Rags to Riches* Shirley played La Belle Diaperina, a chanteuse at the Lullaby Lobster Palace. She wore a Gay Nineties hat and show-girl costume, did her first screen tap dance and sang her first movie song—"She's Only a Bird in a Gilded Cage."

Toward the end of 1932 Shirley was lent by Educational to Tower Productions for *The Red-Haired Alibi*. She played the daughter of a gangster in trouble with the law, who uses his girlfriend as an alibi when she becomes interested in the Shirley character. It was a small role but added a real feature film to Gertrude Temple's list of Shirley's credits.

WAR BABIES

Produced by Jack Hays; directed by Charles Lamont.

Shirley Temple, *Charmaine*; Georgie Smith, *soldier*; Eugene Butler, *soldier*.

THE RUNT PAGE

Produced by Jack Hays; directed by Roy La Verne.

Shirley Temple, *Lulu Parsnips*; Georgie Smith, *Raymond Bunion*.

PIE COVERED WAGON

Produced and written by Jack Hays; directed by Charles Lamont; photographed by Dwight Warren.

Shirley Temple, *captive*; Georgie Smith, *rescuer*; Cowboys and Indians.

GLAD RAGS TO RICHES

Produced by Jack Hays; directed by Charles Lamont.

Shirley Temple, *La Belle Diaperina*; Eugene Butler, *her boyfriend*; Marilyn Granas, Georgie Smith.

THE RED-HAIRED ALIBI

Capitol Films release for Tower Production; directed by Christy Cabanne; screenplay by Edward T. Lowe, from a story by Wilson Collison.

Myrna Kennedy, *Lynn Monith*; Theodore von Eltz, *Trent Travers*; Grant Withers, *Bob Shelton*; Shirley Temple, *Gloria*.

1933

Despite her feature film debut, Shirley went right back to Educational to do four more Baby Burlesks. In *Kid's Last Fight*, a Jack Dempsey spoof, she was kidnapped in an attempt to get the boxer to throw the championship fight. She's rescued just in time. In *Polly-tix in Washington* Shirley portrayed a wealthy gold-digger (in two-piece black lace undies) attempting to elect a cowboy politician to office. In *Kid 'n' Hollywood*, perhaps the best of the eight Burlesks, Shirley played a former beauty contest winner now scrubbing movie soundstage floors. The temperamental star is replaced by the scrubwoman and is molded by director Frightwig Von Stumblebum into "the incomparable Morelegs Sweet Trick," an unsubtle play on Marlene Dietrich.

Kid 'n' Africa, a satire of *Trader Horn* and *Tarzan and His Mate*, was last in the series, the most offensive, and the one Mrs. Black had to pray her Ghanaian admirers would never see; it

As he usually was in *The Baby Burlesks*, Georgie Smith was Shirley's fella in *The Pie-Covered Wagon*.

Shirley is captured by Indians in *Pie-Covered Wagon*, a spoof of *The Covered Wagon*.

represents a white man's view of black Africa and black Africans in the most 1930s-movie-stereotypical terms. She plays Madame Cradlebait, a missionary sent to civilize the cannibals. She is captured by the cannibals and put in a large pot to boil, until she is rescued by "Tarzan," whom she later marries.

Shirley graduated to two-reel shorts at Educational, a series called "Frolics of Youth," for which she was paid fifteen dollars a day or fifty dollars a picture. In her first of three, *Merrily Yours*, Shirley was a little sister who disrupts her brother's household chores—he wants to finish in a hurry, go to the dance and meet a new girl. Then she appeared in another two-reeler, part of Educational's Andy Clyde series, called *Dora's Dunkin' Doughnuts*. A doughnut shop in money trouble is saved by the young woman proprietor's invention of a special dunking doughnut. Her fiance, a teacher played by Andy Clyde, a

Scottish veteran of Mack Sennett comedies, and his music class promote the doughnuts on radio. Shirley steals the picture as one of his younger pupils, breaking up the radio show with a "Ha-cha-cha" ad lib.

Appearances in two more feature films capped the year 1933 for Shirley. Paramount's *To the Last Man* was a Zane Grey western starring Randolph Scott about a range war between two families. Shirley played the daughter of Gail Patrick and Barton MacLane. In Universal's *Out All Night* she played a child checked in a nursery in a department store; ZaSu Pitts played the nursery supervisor, instantly became Shirley's champion, and later became her friend and neighbor.

KID'S LAST FIGHT

Produced by Jack Hays; directed by Charles Lamont.

113

Glad Rags to Riches gave Shirley, as La Belle Diaperina, her first screen song: "She's Only a Bird in a Gilded Cage."

. . . and her first backup chorus boys.

Shirley Temple, *Girlfriend;* Georgie Smith, *Diaper Dampsy;* Sidney Kilbrick, *Thug.*

KID 'N' HOLLYWOOD

Produced by Jack Hays; directed by Charles Lamont.

Shirley Temple, *Morelegs Sweet Trick;* Georgie Smith, *Frightwig Von Stumblebum.*

POLLY-TIX IN WASHINGTON

Produced by Jack Hays; directed by Charles Lamont.

Shirley Temple, *Gold-digger;* Georgie Smith, *Cowboy Politician;* Marilyn Granas, *Maid.*

KID 'N' AFRICA

Produced by Jack Hays; directed by Charles Lamont.

Shirley Temple, *Madame Cradlebait;* Danny Boone Jr., *Diaperzan;* Cannibals.

MERRILY YOURS

Produced by Jack Hays; written and directed by Charles Lamont; photographed by Dwight Warren.

Junior Coughlin, *Sonny Rogers;* Kenneth Howell, *Harry Vanderpool;* Mary Blackford, *Phyllis Dean;* Shirley Temple, *Mary Lou Rogers;* Sidney Miller, *Harry's stooge;* Harry Myers, *Mr. Rogers;* Helene Chadwick, *Mrs. Rogers.*

DORA'S DUNKIN' DOUGHNUTS

Produced by Jack Hays; directed by Harry J. Edwards; story and dialogue by Ernest Pagano and Ewart Adamson; musical numbers by Alfonse Corelli.

116

She didn't always smile—even in *Baby Burlesks*—but even pensive she had dimples.

Merna Kennedy was the *Red-Haired Alibi* in Shirley's first feature film, 1932.

Four-year-old Shirley's footage in *Red-Haired Alibi* was small compared to that of stars Theodo von Eltz, Grant Withers and Merna Kennedy, but it added up to a breakthrough to the big time.

117

The floor-scrubbing ex-beauty queen is about to become More Legs Sweet Trick in *Kid 'n' Hollywood.*

Charles Lamont, who directed *The Baby Burlesks,* shows Shirley the proper camera angle for More Legs Sweet Trick.

Marilyn Granas, as her maid, attends Shirley the hip-high hooker in *Polly-tix in Washington.*

Eric von Stroheim was unsubtly satirized on top of the Fairbanks footprints outside Grauman's Chinese Theatre in *Kid 'n' Hollywood.*

In the part Shirley was potential cannibal fodder; fortunately for her and the United States *Kid 'n' Africa* was never shown in Ghana.

Even in a bit role in the two-reeler *Dora's Dunkin' Donuts*, starring funnyman Andy Clyde, Shirley held center stage.

Madame Cradlebait the missionary, in *Kid 'n' Africa*.

Florence Gill, *Barnyard Nightingale*; Fern Emmett, *Mrs. Zilch*; Balnche Payson, *Mrs. Blotts*; Georgia O'Dell, *Mrs. Ipswick*; Andy Clyde, *Schoolteacher*; Shirley Temple and other "Meglin Kids," *pupils*.

TO THE LAST MAN

Paramount Pictures; directed by Henry Hathaway; screenplay by Jack Cunningham, based on the novel by Zane Grey.

Randolph Scott, *Lynn Hayden*; Esther Ralston, *Ellen Colby*; Shirley Temple, *Mary Standing*; Buster Crabbe, *Bill Hayden*; Noah Beery, *Jed Colby*; Barton MacLane, *Neil Standing*; Gail Patrick, *Ann Hayden Standing*.

OUT ALL NIGHT

Universal; directed by Sam Taylor; screenplay by William Anthony McGuire; based on a story by Tim Whalen.

Slim Summerville, *Ronald Colgate*; ZaSu Pitts, *Bonny*; Laura Hope Crews, *Mrs. Colgate*; Billy Barty, Shirley Temple, Philip Purdy, *Children*.

1934

Shirley finished up at Educational (which went out of business shortly after she left) with two more "Frolics of Youth" as the little sister to Junior Coughlin. In *Pardon My Pups* a real spaniel, Queenie, co-starred. In *Managed Money* the Junior (Sonny) character and a friend go prospecting in the desert to raise money for military school. They meet the school's owner and he enrolls them. A Paramount two-reeler entitled *New Deal Rhythm* was Shirley's next project. The musical featurette co-starred Charles "Buddy" Rogers and Marjorie Main, and Shirley's bit was intended as a screen test.

At 20th Century-Fox she went unbilled as a sharecropper's daughter in *Carolina*, the filmed version of the play by Paul Green, *The House of Connelly*. But the three leads—Janet Gaynor, Lionel Barrymore and Robert Young—were to co-star with her in future films. Shirley was also barely visible in Warner Bros.–First National's *Mandalay*, with Kay Francis. Her last two films in other than leading roles were at Fox: *Now I'll Tell*, a melodrama based on the life of New York gambler Arnold Rothstein, and *Change of Heart*, based on Kathleen Norris's *Manhattan Love Song*.

Stand Up and Cheer was Shirley's big breakthrough in movies. Having passed her Fox audition by singing "Baby, Take a Bow," she recorded the song for the soundtrack after just two weeks of specialized training. She was five years old. The film, based on an idea by Will Rogers, centered on a mythical United States Secretary of Amusements who would cheer the country up during the Depression by organizing government-sponsored vaudeville acts. Shirley's number, with James Dunn, was such a smash that she landed her first contract. She was a billable movie star, and the short films and bit parts were a thing of the past.

PARDON MY PUPS

Produced by Jack Hays; directed by Charles Lamont; screenplay by Ewart Adamson, based on the story "Mild Oats," by Florence Ryerson and Colin Clements.

Junior Coughlin, *Sonny*; Shirley Temple, *Mary Lou*; Kenneth Howell, *Harry Vanderpool*; Queenie, *Spaniel*.

MANAGED MONEY

Produced by Jack Hays; directed by Charles Lamont.

Shirley Temple, *Mary Lou*; Frank (Junior) Coughlin, *Sonny*; Harry Myers, *Friend*; Huntley Gordon, *Schoolmaster*.

NEW DEAL RHYTHM

Paramount.

Charles "Buddy" Rogers, Marjorie Main, Shirley Temple.

CAROLINA

Fox; directed by Henry King; screenplay by Reginald Berkeley, based on the play "The House of Connelly," by Paul Green.

Janet Gaynor, *Joanna*; Lionel Barrymore, *Bob Connelly*; Robert Young, *Will Connelly*; Stepin Fetchit, *Scipio*.

Pardon My Pups was a 1933 two-reeler that got Shirley her audition for *Stand Up and Cheer.*

"Little sister" watches Dorothy Ward and Kenneth Howell bathe Queenie.

Shirley played the little sister in four Educational two-reelers, here in *Managed Money*.

Which got her to the desert for tur-
tle—watching with Junior Coughlin,
Harry Myers and Huntley Gordon.

Or, how to help your big brother and his pal get to military school in *Managed Money*.

Janet Gaynor, the first actress to win an Oscar (1928), was the star of *Carolina* and *Change of Heart*, but was soon to be overtaken by Shirley—a bit player in those films—in popularity. Temple and Gaynor were next door neighbors on the Fox lot, and sisters under the dimples.

The big break came in *Stand Up And Cheer* when Shirley sang and danced "Baby, Take a Bow" with James Dunn. The red polka-dot dress became an instant fashion hit with little girls.

MANDALAY

Warner Bros.–First National; directed by Michael Curtiz; screenplay by Austin Parker and Charles Kenyon, based on a story by Paul Hervey Fox.

Kay Francis, *Tanya;* Ricardo Cortez, *Tony Evans;* Warner Oland, *Nick;* Lyle Talbot, *Dr. Gregory Burton.*

NOW I'LL TELL

Fox; directed by Edwin Burke, based on the book by Mrs. Arnold Rothestein.

Spencer Tracy, *Murray Golden;* Helen Twelvetrees, *Virginia;* Alice Faye, *Peggy;* Shirley Temple, *Mary Golden.*

CHANGE OF HEART

Fox; directed by John G. Blystone; screenplay by Sonya Levien, and James Gleason, based on the novel by Kathleen Norris.

Janet Gaynor, *Catherine Furness;* Charles Farrell, *Chris Thring;* Ginger Rogers, *Madge Rountree;* James Dunn, *Mack McGowan;* Shirley Temple, *Shirley.*

STAND UP AND CHEER

Fox; directed by Hamilton McFadden; screenplay by Ralph Spence, based on an outline by Will Rogers and Philip Klein; songs by Lew Brown, Jay Gorney (including "Baby, Take a Bow").

In a modified Girl Scout uniform Shirley Temple led the parade in *Stand Up and Cheer,* in 1934, and from then on never looked back.

129

Shirley as Little Miss Marker.

LITTLE MISS MARKER

Warner Baxter, *Lawrence Cronwell;* Madge Evans, *Mary Adams;* James Dunn, *Jimmy Dugan;* Shirley Temple, *Shirley Dugan;* Stepin Fetchit, *himself;* Aunt Jemima (Tess Gardell), *herself;* John Boles, *himself.*

1934; Paramount; directed by Alexander Hall; screenplay by William R. Lipman, Sam Hellman, Gladys Lehman; based on the story by Damon Runyon.

Adolphe Menjou, *Sorrowful Jones;* Dorothy Dell, *Bangles Carson;* Charles Bickford, *Big Steve;* Shirley Temple, *Miss Marker, Martha, Marky;* Edward Earle, *her father.*

Paramount, which has already had Shirley in *New Deal Rhythm* and *To the Last Man,* was interested in Shirley for the Runyon story, which they had owned for two years and considered rewriting for a boy (Jackie Cooper). Fortunately, they cast Shirley (paying Fox a thousand dollars a week, of which she got only $150); it's one of her best movies, despite a tearjerker plot. A little girl is left by her father as security for a loan. He gambles, loses the money and commits suicide. The gambling house owner keeps the "marker" and makes a home for her. Menjou and Temple were magic together on screen, and friends off it. He played jacks and hide-and-seek with her, and marveled at her craft: "If she were forty years old and on stage all her life she wouldn't have had the time to learn all she knows about acting."

The lovable underworld characters of Runyon spouting hard-boiled dialogue calculated to upset Mrs. Temple ("Aw, lay off me," Shirley tells Dorothy Dell, playing a singer who in another scene says to Shirley, "Scram kid, you're crabbing my act") were a thorough delight despite the mawkish story line, and the movie was an instant hit.

Shirley kibitzes the poker game. Adolphe Menjou appears to resent the intrusion. Lynn Overman looks on.

A new star is born.

Dorothy Dell tries to cajole a pouting Shirley into eating her breakfast.

BABY, TAKE A BOW

1934; Fox, directed by Harry Lachman; screenplay by Philip Klein and E. E. Paramore, Jr., based on the play "Square Crooks" by James R. Judge.

James Dunn, *Eddie Ellison*; Claire Trevor, *Kay Ellison*; Shirley Temple, *Shirley.*

Back home at Fox, and based on the success of *Little Miss Marker* and *Stand Up and Cheer,* Shirley's salary was raised to $1,250 weekly, plus $150 a week for Gertrude as coach and hairdresser. Her home studio used the title of the song from *Stand Up and Cheer* and reteamed her with James Dunn. Dunn plays a gangster trying to go straight and build a good life for his family. He and Shirley sing a duet, "On Accounta I Love You." The movie was pleasant, sentimental and a moneymaker.

James Dunn and Shirley learn their dances for *Baby, Take a Bow.*

Shirley tries to restrain her gangster father from a further criminal act in *Baby, Take A Bow*.

By the time she made *Baby, Take a Bow* Shirley had learned to sit like a lady between takes.

136

On the set Shirley began to learn something about the technical side of film-making too . . .

. . . . thanks to director Harry Lachman.

Shirley, her koala bear, and James Dunn rest setside between takes of *Baby, Take a Bow*.

137

Gary Cooper called Shirley "Wiggle-britches" during *Now and Forever* and she recalled him as "too tall to talk to when he stood up."

NOW AND FOREVER

Cooper (as a con-man and Shirley's daddy) . . .

. . . and Carole Lombard (as the con-man's moll) . . .

1934; Paramount, directed by Henry Hathaway; screenplay by Vincent Lawrence and Sylvia Thalberg, based on a story by Jack Kirkland and Melville Baker.

Gary Cooper, *Jerry Day;* Carole Lombard, *Toni Carstairs;* Shirley Temple, *Penelope Day;* Sir Guy Standing, *Felix Evans;* Dog Buster, *Dachshund.*

At Paramount for one last loanout, Shirley was billed third after the stellar Gary Cooper and Carole Lombard, but still saddled with a criminal father who tries to go straight for her sake. Cooper as the con and Lombard as his doll seems to be walking through the mawkish story, and who can blame them? Shirley smiled, charmed and sang ("The World Owes Me a Living") her way through the movie, but even she couldn't save the impossible, schizoid screenplay. (One scene has Cooper stealing a necklace and hiding it in her teddy bear.)

Off screen, *Now and Forever* was a much happier experience. Shirley adored Gary Cooper, who nicknamed her "Wigglebritches." He taught her to draw, and bought her a teddy bear of her own, which she named Grumpy. When Dorothy Dell, the promising co-star of *Little Miss Marker*, was killed in an automobile accident during the filming of *Now and Forever*, Carole Lombard comforted a distraught Shirley.

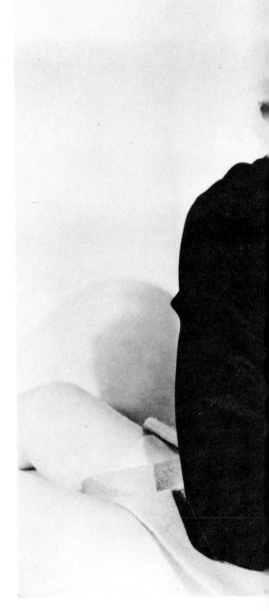

. . . were two of Paramount's most popular stars, but Shirley was the real charmer of *Now and Forever.*

Lionel Barrymore at first resisted working with a child star, but he became grandfatherly to her in real life as well as in *The Little Colonel.*

Forget Astaire-Rogers! The most famous dancing duo in movies was Bill "Bojangles" Robinson and Shirley Temple, here in *The Little Colonel.*

One of the best Robinson-Temple numbers was the stair dance in *The Little Colonel.*

This lobby card for *Our Little Girl* promised more fun than the plot was able to deliver.

OUR LITTLE GIRL

1935; 20th Century-Fox, directed by John Robertson; screenplay by Stephen Avery, Allen Rivkin, Jack Yellen, based on the story "Heaven's Gate" by Florence Leighton Pfalzgraf; song by Paul Francis Webster, Lew Pollack.

Shirley Temple, *Molly Middleton;* Rosemary Ames, *Elsa Middleton;* Joel McCrea, *Dr. Donald Middleton;* Lyle Talbot, *Rolfe Brent;* Poodles Hanneford, *clown, himself.*

One of the soapiest and least interesting of Temple films, *Our Little Girl* has a doctor neglecting his wife and daughter. The wife takes up horseback riding with the rich male neighbor next door. The daughter runs away. The family is reunited and the doctor stops being neglectful. Shirley had endless wardrobe changes and cute closeups.

Shirley and Poodles Hanneford clowned around between scenes.

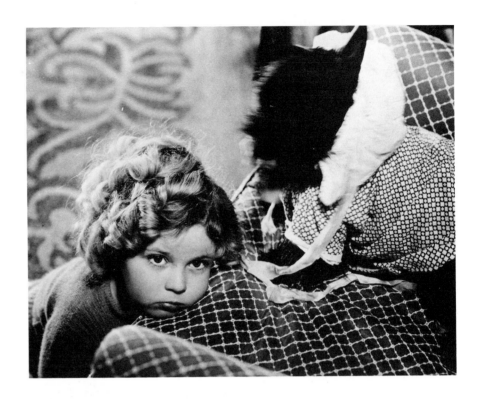

Joel McCrea was too good-looking to be believable as the neglectful daddy.

1935; 20th Century-Fox, directed by Irving Cummings; screenplay by Patterson McNutt and Arthur Beckhard, based on the story "Daddy Longlegs" by Jean Webster; songs by Ray Henderson, Ted Koehler, Edward Heyman, Irving Caesar (nicluding "Animal Crackers," "It's All So New to Me," "When I Grow Up," "The Simple Things," "Curly Top.")

Shirley Temple, *Betsy Blair;* John Boles, *Edward Morgan, orphange trustee;* Rochelle Hudson, *Mary Blair;* Jane Darwell, *Mrs. Denham;* Esther Dale, *Aunt Genevieve;* Arthur Treacher, *Morgan's butler.*

The first of four Temple remakes of Mary Pickford silent films opens with a shot of the back of Shirley's curly head; then we see her turn her head and smile and dimple in almost a minute-long closeup. Thus was abandoned all pretense that Shirley Temple movies were about anything, or indeed anything more than a vehicle for her adorableness. In *Curly Top* Shirley introduced "Animal Crackers (in My Soup)" and "When I Grow Up," danced a hula at a nighttime beach party, and tapped on top of a white piano while John Boles sang the title song. Shirley and her older sister are supposed to be orphans who are rescued by a rich bachelor (Boles) who adopts Shirley and marries the sister. The plot's banality —and tribute to conspicuous consumption on the part of the few remaining rich during the Depression—were lost in the tidal wave of popularity that greeted *Curly Top.*

John Boles rescued Shirley and her older sister from orphanhood in *Curly Top,* an inferior re-make of *Daddy Longlegs,* that nonetheless introduced "Animal Crackers in my Soup."

Shirley happily watched romance bloom between John Boles and Rochelle Hudson . . .

. . . and danced on his piano.

158

Arthur Treacher played the butler in *Curly Top* for his first of four appearances in Temple films, and when the star beckoned he bent.

The littlest rebel.

THE LITTLEST REBEL

1935; 20th Century-Fox, produced by Darryl F. Zanuck; directed by David Butler; screenplay by Edwin Burke and Harry Tugend, based on the play by Edward Peple.

Shirley Temple, *Virginia Houston Cary (Virgie)*; John Boles, *Capt. Herbert Cary (Confederate)*; Jack Holt, *Colonel Morrison (Union)*; Karen Morely, *Mrs. Cary*; Bill Robinson, *Uncle Bill, Cary slave*; Bessie Lyle, *Mammy*; Frank McGlynn, Sr., *President Lincoln.*

Despite the similarity in title and setting to *The Little Colonel* and Shirley's reteaming with Bill Robinson, *The Littlest Rebel* is much more dramatically worthy than its predecessor. Beautifully photographed, *The Littlest Rebel* is set during the Civil War and features Shirley in a blackface disguise at one point. She dances and sings "Polly Wolly Doodle" with Robinson on the sidewalk and sings "Believe Me, If All Those Endearing Young Charms" by herself. She goes north to Washington, where, in hoopskirt and ruffles, she pleads with Abraham Lincoln for the release of her father, who has been captured by Union soldiers while visiting his dying wife. (Shirley seldom had living mothers in her movies.) Her sobbing pleas are interrupted frequently to eat slices of apple that President Lincoln has been peeling. Off camera the worldly seven-year-old Miss Temple discussed the scene with associate producer Buddy DeSylva: "Of course the pardon has to be granted. We can't make a heavy out of Lincoln."

The littlest rebel tries to be brave as her Confederate captain daddy (John Boles) leaves for the front, as Bill Robinson and Willie Best look on.

161

Golden-haired Shirley in blackface fooled absolutely no one, least of all Union Soldier Guinn Williams.

162

The Southern family (including Bessie Lyle as Mammy, Karen Morley as the mother and Bill Robinson as a senior slave) wait to welcome the master home from the front.

Look away, Dixieland.

By 1936, and *Captain January*, Shirley's billing was not only above the title, it was bigger than the title.

CAPTAIN JANUARY

1936; 20th Century-Fox, produced by Darryl F. Zanuck; directed by David Butler; screenplay by Sam Hellman, Gladys Lehman, Harry Tugend, based on the story by Laura E. Richards; songs by Lew Polalck, Sidney D. Mitchell, Jack Yellen (including "Early Bird," "At the Codfish Ball," "The Right Somebody To Love)."

Shirley Temple, *Star;* Guy Kibbee, *Captain January;* Slim Summerville, *Captain Nazro;* Buddy Ebsen, *Paul Rogers;* Jane Darwell, *Eliza Croft;* Jerry Tucker, *Cyril Morgan;* John Carradine, *East Indian.*

Shirley's first release in 1936—and the first since the reorganization of the $54 million 20th Century-Fox of which she was the single most valuable asset—turned out to be one of the best movies she ever made. Based on the 1890 Laura E. Richards story *The Lighthouse at Cape Tempest, Captain January* was the story of a poor foundling named Star (Shirley) who was washed up on the New England seashore and taken in by a kindly lighthouse keeper (Guy Kibbee), but pursued by a truant officer. ("Cap! Cap! I don't want to go!" Shirley shouted.)

Her songs in *Captain January* included "Early Bird," with which she awoke in the morning, and "The Right Somebody to Love." A dance with Buddy Ebsen, "At the Codfish Ball," is among the best numbers she did in film. A camera tracked along a wooden street following the pair as they danced over stacks of boxes and barrels and up and down wooden stairs. During the filming of this sequence, Shirley had to climb a forty-five-foot stairway while a camera crane moved up beside her, catching her lines each time she turned on the stairs—timing the line exactly to the turn. Shirley never missed the synchronization once. With Kibbee and Slim Summerville, Shirley did a three-part version of the sextet from "Lucia." (Her mother had been an opera singer.) Ebsen, TV's "Barnaby Jones" in the late 1970s, remembered himself as "the new boy in town and Shirley the established star" in *Captain January,* where he learned movie techniques from her.

Shirley was vain enough about stardom; when a minor child player, Jerry Tucker, was getting applause on the set for a good job of acting in a schoolroom scene, Shirley sat on a small chair out of camera range, her eyes flashing with jealousy. Her scene following his was a full page of dialogue. As with all long speeches David Butler, the director, had planned to break the scene between a medium shot and a closeup. But when Shirley began her speech Butler let the camera run through the entire long monologue, which Shirley, to regain her position, was delivering without a mistake. In fact, Shirley's only problem in *Captain January* was that her baby teeth kept falling out and she had to wear temporary false caps on camera.

On the release of *Captain January* in early 1936 critics divided as they always did on Shirley Temple movies. "Neither epic, romance, nor extravaganza," *Time* wrote, "it is designed solely as its star's vehicle. As an item of entertainment *Captain January* depends entirely upon the fact that Shirley Temple appears in almost every sequence, grinning, sobbing, dancing, singing, wriggling, pattering downstairs or spitting on her pinafore as the scenario requires. That this is entirely as it should be, in the opinion of U.S. cinemaddicts, was proved by the reception of the picture. *Captain January* smashed box-office records in Milwaukee, Portland, Me., Dayton, Richmond, Cincinnati, Boston and Baltimore." Frank Nugent of *The New York Times,* however, denounced the movie's "moss-covered script."

Veterans Slim Summerville, Shirley Temple, and Guy Kibbee sing to novice Buddy Ebsen.

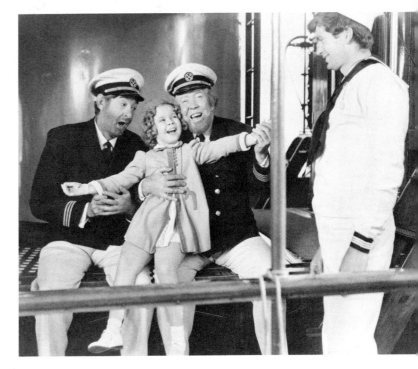

Shirley and Buddy Ebsen danced across town to the lively song "At the Codfish Ball."

166

They were followed across docks, steps, decks and barrels by a dancing camera, in Jack Donohue's inventive choreography.

Shirley practices her hula dance for *Captain January,* while Buddy Ebsen strums his uke, on Malibu Beach.

Guy Kibbee was *Captain January*.

Jack, Shirley and Alice dressed for their tap finale "I Love a Military Man."

POOR LITTLE RICH GIRL

1936; 20th Century-Fox, produced by Darryl F. Zanuck; directed by Irving Cummings; screenplay by Sam Hellman, Gladys Lehman, Harry Tugend, based on stories by Eleanor Gates; songs by Mack Gordon, Harry Revel (including "But Definitely," "You've Got to Eat Your Spinach Baby," "When I'm with You.")

Shirley Temple, *Barbara Barry*; Alice Faye, *Jerry Dolan*; Jack Haley, *Jimmy Dolan*; Gloria Stuart, *Margaret Allen*; Jane Darwell, *Woodward*; Michael Whalen, *Richard Barry.*

When *Poor Little Rich Girl* was released, Nugent of *The New York Times* didn't like it any better than he had *Captain January.* He lamented unnecessarily on behalf of co-stars Jack Haley and Alice Faye: "Short of becoming a defeated candidate for Vice President, we can think of no better way of guaranteeing one's anonymity than appearing in the moppet's films."

Shirley once again played a girl whose widowed and rich father was too busy with business to take care of her. She hooks up with two vaudeville performers (Faye and Haley), becomes a radio star and, by doing commercials for her father's soap company, becomes reunited with him.

Poor Little Rich Girl had a lot less plot than Pickford's 1916 version, but had some nice songs (Shirley's "When I'm with You" and "Oh My Goodness" and Alice's "But Definitely") and, in the making, the first indication that Shirley was less than a perfect performer. "I Love a Military Man," an obviously tacked-on tap number, was a little fast and intricate even for Shirley, and Jack Haley remembered that "they dubbed in Shirley's taps but didn't tell Mrs. Temple. They shot it with her, then told Alice and me to come back later and do it again. At the preview Mrs. Temple was boasting, 'Did you hear those taps? Could they have been any clearer? And you said Shirley couldn't do it.'"

Hopeful radio entertainers Alice Faye and Jack Haley befriend a lonely Shirley in *Poor Little Rich Girl.*

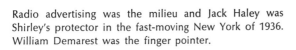
Faye, Temple and Haley stroll the Fox lot as if they own it—and the middle one just about did.

Radio advertising was the milieu and Jack Haley was Shirley's protector in the fast-moving New York of 1936. William Demarest was the finger pointer.

Radio was a star of *Poor Little Rich Girl*, too, reuniting Shirley and her neglectful father.

Michael Whalen, who played her rich, neglectful father in *Poor Little Rich Girl*, poses with Shirley for a publicity still.

Dimples (the film in production was
called *The Bowery Princess*) slept
where she could.

DIMPLES

1936; 20th Century-Fox, produced by Darryl F. Zanuck; directed by William A. Seiter; screenplay by Arthur Sheekman and Nat Perrin; songs by Jimmy McHugh, Ted Koehler (including "He was a Dandy and She Was a Belle" and "Get on Board").

Shirley Temple, *Sylvia Dolores (Dimples) Appleby;* Frank Morgan, *Professor Appleby;* Helen Westley, *Mrs. Caroline Draw;* Stepin Fetchit, *Cicero;* John Carradine, *Richards.*

In October 1936 Nugent denounced *Dimples* even more vehemently. "The Shirley Temple for President Club reconvened yesterday and displayed flattering attention to their candidate's latest assault upon the nation's maternal instinct," Nugent wrote in his *Times* review. "*Dimples* is its apt title, apt because it is just another word for Little Miss Precocity and does not pretend to describe the story material it employs. Why they bother with titles, or with plots either, is beyond us."

In *Dimples*, which was set in the New York City of 1850 and tried for a Dickensian flavor, Shirley was upstaged for the first time in one of her starring pictures. Frank Morgan, later the Wizard of Oz, played her Micawberesque grandfather with such energy and fun as to render Shirley, as the street urchin who becomes a Broadway star, faltering and hollow. The unabated box-office success of *Dimples*, however, caused Zanuck and the rest of 20th Century-Fox to worry less about the money crises occasioned by Will Rogers' death in a plane crash.

Dimples was darling and Dickensian, and Shirley was a New York street urchin who became a Broadway star as Little Eva in the first production of *Uncle Tom's Cabin.*

Dimples liked dolls as much as its star but was far less able to afford them. (With Frank Morgan and Billy Gilbert).

Frank Morgan, who three years later would play the title role in *The Wizard of Oz*, played Shirley's grandfather, a musical street thief of the 1850s. He was the first co-star to steal a Temple picture.

As the orphaned daughter of missionaries in China, Shirley sang good songs well ("Goodnight, My Love," "That's What I Want for Christmas"), spoke Chinese and imitated Al Jolson, Eddie Cantor and Ginger Rogers.

STOWAWAY

1936; 20th Century-Fox, produced by Darryl F. Zanuck; directed by William A. Seiter; screenplay by William Conselman, Arthur Sheekman, Nat Perrin, based on the story by Sam Engel; songs by Mack Gordon, Harry Revel, Irving Caesar (including "Goodnight, My Love," "You Gotta S-M-I-L-E," "One Never Knows, Does One?" "That's What I Want for Christmas").

Shirley Temple, *Ching-Ching;* Robert Young, *Tommy Randall;* Alice Faye, *Susan Parker;* Helen Westley, *Mrs. Hope;* Arthur Treacher, *Atkins;* Eugene Pallette, *The Colonel.*

Stowaway, her last 1936 film, had Shirley an orphan again, the daughter of missionaries in China who were killed by bandits. She is adopted by a rich playboy, of course. For the picture she learned and spoke Mandarin Chinese. Her co-stars were Robert Young and Alice Faye (who got two of the film's excellent songs: "Goodnight, My Love" and "One Never Knows, Does One?"). Shirley promoted a romance between Young and Faye, and did imitations of Eddie Cantor, Ginger Rogers (with a male doll in black tie attached to her toes) and Al Jolson singing "Mammy." The picture cleaned up.

Three teachers kept Shirley occupied four hours every school day. Her regular teacher, Frances Klampt ("Klammie"), was joined during *Stowaway* by Bessie Nyi, teaching Chinese for the picture, and Paula Walling, who taught Shirley French.

179

Robert Young was the rich playboy
who adopted Shirley . . .

. . . She, in turn, pointed the way to a romance with Alice Faye.

WEE WILLIE WINKIE

1937; 20th Century-Fox, produced by Darryl F. Zanuck; directed by John Ford; screenplay by Ernest Pascal and Julien Josephson, based on the story by Rudyard Kipling.

Shirley Temple, *Priscilla Williams;* Victor McLaglen, *Sergeant MacDuff;* C. Aubrey Smith, *Colonel Williams;* Cesar Romero, *Khoda Khan;* Constance Collier, *Mrs. Allardyce;* June Lang, *Joyce Williams.*

In keeping with her real-life tomboy interests, one of Shirley's favorite movies was *Wee Willie Winkie,* based on Kipling, directed by Ford, and of course originally conceived for a boy. "In the movie I was a real bossy girl," she remembered. "I marched, drilled, did the manual of arms. I had a wooden gun. It was wonderful." The plot had her visiting her army grandfather in India, befriending a prisoner who led rebellious natives and negotiating for peace between the two warring factors.

Darryl Zanuck conceived the notion of pairing her with John Ford. Her three strong male co-stars were Victor McLaglen, Cesar Romero and C. Aubrey Smith. (Her favorites remained, however, her first, James Dunn, Bill Robinson, and Gary Cooper—"he was so tall I barely ever talked to him unless he was sitting down, he was so kind and bashful.") Shirley not only liked the picture for its military flavor, she also liked Ford: "Outwardly he is a rugged person," she said, "but inside he's kindly and even sentimental."

Ford, who after working with her gave her the sobriquet "One-Take Temple," recalled how Zanuck had begun to tamper with the formula for Shirley's movies: "One day Darryl said, 'I'm going to give you something to scream about. I'm going to put you together with Shirley Temple.' He thought that combination would make me and everybody howl. I said, 'Great,' and we just went out an made the picture. It made a lot of money." Ford and Temple stayed friends until his death, and he became Susan's godfather.

Fox advertised its biggest attraction in her latest appearance with a huge billboard at one end of the studio.

McLaglen and his wee recruit were right on target.

For all the right reasons (director Ford's unmistakable feel for place and battle action, spectacle and adult-style human relationships) *Wee Willie Winkie* was Shirley's favorite of her own films.

184

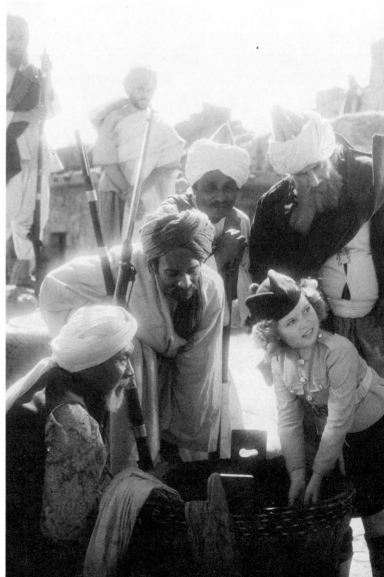

Romero was Khoda Khan, Victor McLaglen (center) was
Sergeant MacDuff and June Lang, Shirley's mother, in *Wee
Willie Winkie.*

185

HEIDI

1937; 20th Century-Fox produced by Darryl F. Zanuck; directed by Allan Dwan; screenplay by Walter Ferris and Julien Josephson, based on the story by Johanna Spyri.

Shirley Temple, *Heidi*; Jean Hersholt, *Grandfather*; Arthur Treacher, *Andrews*; Helen Westley, *Blind Anna*; Pauline Moore, *Elsa*; Delmar Watson, *Peter*; Sidney Blackmer, *Herr Sesemann*.

Director Allan Dwan, in his nineties, recalled that when he was put together with Shirley for *Heidi* "she was waning. She'd had her peak and was sliding. Zanuck would like to have made a trade, but nobody was interested, and I liked to avoid children, especially those who were over. In a kind of left-handed way he gave me *Heidi* and said, 'see what you can do with it.' *Heidi's* a very down story, stiff and heavy, but Zanuck loosened the purse strings a little. We got to use Lake Arrowhead locations for the Alps—and a lot of tricks. She helped invent the dream sequence where she's in Holland because she thought that way—she knew it was a good spot for a musical number."

Heidi could have been written for Shirley Temple at the crossroads of her career. She was now nearly four feet tall—against three feet-two inches in 1934, and her hair was soon to be parted into two pony tails, another sign of advancing age. The desentimentalized and jazzed-up *Heidi* and *Wee Willie Winkie*, her only two films in 1937, were enough to make her number one at the box office for the third year in a row. Still, the one-year-old *Life* magazine worried: "What's to become of Shirley Temple? She has lost some of her early prettiness and all of her babyish cuteness, but has gained enough acting tricks to leave her with a full quota of charm."

Arthur Treacher as the butler (what else?) ushers Heidi into her new life in the big city.

187

Filming *Heidi* at Lake Arrowhead was a picnic for Shirley, Jean Hersholt (far right) and other members of the cast.

189

Radio singing was also central to the plot in *Rebecca of Sunnybrook Farm*—and for exactly the same reason it had been in *Poor Little Rich Girl:* it reconciled Shirley to her dad.

REBECCA OF SUNNYBROOK FARM

1938; 20th Century-Fox, produced by Darryl F. Zanuck; directed by Allan Dwan; screenplay by Karl Tunberg and Don Ettlinger, based on the story by Kate Douglas Wiggin; songs by Sidney Mitchell and Lew Pollack, Mack Gordon and Harry Revel, Jack Yellen and Samuel Pokrass (including "Alone with You," "If I Had One Wish to Make," "Come and Get Your Happiness").

Shirley Temple, *Rebecca Winstead;* Randolph Scott, *Anthony Kent;* Jack Haley, *Orville Smithers;* Gloria Stuart, *Gwenn Warren;* Phyllis Brooks, *Lola Lee;* Helen Westley, *Aunt Miranda Wilkins;* Slim Summerville, *Homer Busby;* Bill Robinson, *Aloysius;* Raymond Scott Quintet, *as themselves;* Alan Dinehart, *Purvis;* J. Edward Bromberg, *Dr. Hill;* Dixie Dunbar, *Receptionist;* Paul Hurst, *Mug;* William Demarest, *Henry Kipper;* Ruth Gillette, *Melba;* Paul Harvey, *Cyrus Bartlett;* Clarence Hummel Wilson, *Jake Singer;* Sam Hayes, Gary Breckner, Carroll Nye, *Radio announcers;* Franklin Pangborn, *Hamilton Montmarcy.*

Another Mary Pickford remake, also directed by Dwan (who had directed Pickford in 1915's *A Girl of Yesterday*), *Rebecca of Sunnybrook Farm* found the familiar original story in a shambles but Shirley at the top of her form. "Any actress who can dominate a Zanuck musical with Jack Haley, Gloria Stuart, Phyllis Brooks, Helen Westley, Slim Summerville, Bill Robinson, Randolph Scott, Franklin Pangborn, etc. can dominate the world," *Variety* wrote.

Rebecca left no stone unturned when it came to milking the old Shirley Temple formula. Her new songs included "Come and Get Your Happiness." The film's finale was a tap dance with Bill Robinson done to "The Parade of the Wooden Soldiers," and both veterans were in snappy form. She sang, in the guise of Rebecca making her radio debut, a medley of her earlier hits, including "On the Good Ship Lollipop" and "When I'm with You."

Whatever happened to Randolph Scott? Gloria Stuart knew that Temple was going to steal the movie from both of them, and sure enough she did.

Even farewells were danced in the Temple-Robinson flicks.

192

Pros like Scott, Stuart and Helen Westley were as incidental to the Temple vehicles as the Kate Wiggins story from which the title and little else was taken.

Not just another dancing partner, but George Murphy, a future Republican senator from California, deferred to his ten-year-old co-star in *Little Miss Broadway*.

LITTLE MISS BROADWAY

1938; 20th Century-Fox, produced by Darryl F. Zanuck; directed by Irving Cummings; screenplay by Harry Tugend, Jack Yellen; songs, Walter Bullock, Harold Spina (including "Be Optimistic," "How Can I Thank You?" "We Should Be Together").

Shirley Temple, *Betsy Brown*; George Murphy, *Roger Wendling*; Jimmy Durante, *Jimmy Clayton*; Phyllis Brooks, *Barbara Shea*; Edna May Oliver, *Sarah Wendling*; Jane Darwell, *Miss Hutchins*.

An orphan living at a hotel for theatrical performers, Shirley joins in battle with her co-tenants against a rich neighbor complaining about the noise. *Little Miss Broadway* was written just for Shirley, even to the point of explaining her new hairdo: "I used to have curls all over my head, but they were a lot of trouble." There was no explaining away her new seventy-one-pound plumpness and her four-feet-three-inch height. But fortunately the film also had a smooth George Murphy dancing a beautiful duet with Shirley to "We Should Be Together"; one of the best of all Temple songs, "Be Optimistic"; Edna May Oliver, Jimmy Durante and "Swing Me an Old-Fashioned Song" to enliven it.

Murphy remembered that during filming Shirley —now ten—"would pop out of the damnedest places to see if you had your police badge on, and raised between $2,000 and $3,000 from twenty-five cent fines." He also remembered "giving her" their scenes together. "Some of the critics mentioned this, but I never tried to compete; I always deferred to her."

Jimmy Durante and Shirley dance their evidence in the court of crabby judge Claude Gillingwater, in *Little Miss Broadway*.

In court, Shirley saves the denizens of a theatrical hotel from eviction.

JUST AROUND
THE CORNER

1938; 20th Century-Fox, produced by Darryl F. Zanuck; directed by Irving Cummings; screenplay by Ethel Hill, J. P. McEvoy, Darrell Ware, based on the novel "Lucky Penny" by Paul Gerard Smith.

Shirley Temple, *Penny Hale;* Charles Farrell, *Jeff Hale;* Joan Davis, *Kitty;* Bill Robinson, *Corporal Jones;* Franklin Pangborn, *Waters;* Bert Lahr, *Gus.*

Unlike a Stradivarius, Shirley's (or Mrs. Temple's) instrument was clearly not improving with age. Neither were her scripts. In *Just around the Corner,* Shirley's formerly rich widowed father—again—was reduced to being a maintenance man at an apartment house; Shirley helps him get a better job and a wife. Despite a first-rate cast and a final Temple–Robinson dance duet, "I Love to Walk in the Rain," the film foundered at the box office. *The New York Times* opined: "It can't be old age, but it does look like weariness." Shirley had pulled out all stops and even indulged in a Jane Withers ploy, acting out one of her fantasies by pummelling her picture playmates with a toy machine gun and saying, "I guess that'll teach you a lesson—you can't fool a G-woman."

Riches to rags to riches again with Charles Farrell and Shirley—but she'd done it better before.

George Temple smoked a pipe, and Shirley often lit it for him, so she had no trouble doing the same for her screen father, Charles Farrell, during the rehearsal for *Just Around The Corner*.

Unfortunately, the plot of *Just Around the Corner* was as likely to hit target as Bert Lahr's and Shirley's guns in this scene.

Just Around the Corner was Bill Robinson's fourth and last Temple film.

Shirley's last great success as a child star was also her most beautifully mounted movie—a mini-opera dream sequence is alone worth the price of admission. Here she wakes from the dream with some of its remnants in her garret. Mary Nash accuses her and Sybil Jason of stealing the rich clothing.

THE LITTLE PRINCESS

1939; 20th Century-Fox, produced by Darryl F. Zanuck; directed by Walter Lang; screenplay by Ethel Hill, Walter Ferris, based on the novel by Frances Hodgson Burnett. Filmed in Technicolor.

Shirley Temple, *Sara Crewe;* Richard Greene, *Geoffrey Hamilton;* Anita Louise, *Rose;* Ian Hunter, *Captain Crewe;* Cesar Romero, *Ram Dass;* Arthur Treacher, *Bertie Minchin.*

Twentieth Century-Fox turned to Technicolor and a big budget ($1.5 million) to shore up their falling star for *The Little Princess,* yet a fourth Pickford silent triumph, based on the Frances Hodgson Burnett novel and set in England in 1899. The story was a perfect Pickford–Temple

costume fantasy: Daddy marches off to the Boer War (Mommy, naturally, is dead), having spoiled his daughter princess-style. A schoolmistress forces Shirley to work like a servant. No less a personage than Queen Victoria is brought in to sort it all out. Arthur Treacher, a four-time Temple co-star and the prototypical butler, sang and danced with Shirley, and Anita Louise and Richard Greene were an attractive young romantic couple.

The Little Princess was a deserving critical success (in many respects, including photography and production values, it's Shirley's finest film), but the box-office success in the children's fantasy department in 1939 was *The Wizard of Oz,* and Judy Garland was the future as Shirley Temple was the past. (Ironically, Shirley had been considered for the role of Dorothy in *The Wizard* two years before.)

Queen Victoria (Beryl Mercer) was one of the reasons *The Little Princess* worked so well as a Temple fantasy film.

204

It was late Victorian England, there were lavish costumes—and technicolor for the first time. Anita Louise (over Shirley's right shoulder) and Arthur Treacher were on hand and Shirley was the perfect little princess, just as Mary Pickford had been.

SUSANNA OF THE MOUNTIES

1939; 20th Century-Fox, produced by Darryl F. Zanuck; directed by William A. Seiter; screenplay by Robert Ellis and Helen Logan, based on the story by Fidel La Barba and Walter Ferris, and the book by Muriel Denison.

Shirley Temple, *Susannah Sheldon;* Randolph Scott, *Monty Montague;* Margaret Lockwood, *Vicky Standing;* Martin Good Rider, *Little Chief;* J. Farrell MacDonald, *Pat O'Hannegan;* Victor Jory, *Wolf Pelt.*

As the only survivor of an Indian massacre, Shirley is rescued by mounted police; she helps them to improve relations with the Indians. *Susannah of the Mounties* was the last movie in Shirley's seven-year association with 20th Century-Fox to make money. At the age of eleven she was given a preadolescent semi-romantic interest in Martin Good Rider, a pureblooded Blackfoot Indian boy. But her mini-squaw character in this banal melodrama of the Northwest was unsympathetic, and she was limited to one pathetic song and dance: "I'll Teach You a Waltz."

As the lone survivor of a wagon-train massacre, eleven-year-old Shirley (Susannah) becomes Golden Hawk, the Little Spirit of the Sun.

Randolph Scott, as Monty, the Canadian Mountie, adopts Shirley, in her last Fox child film to make money.

Russell and Temple sneak toward the Land of Luxury, whereas Judy Garland and her pals had struck out determinedly for Oz.

THE BLUE BIRD

1940; 20th Century-Fox, produced by Darryl F. Zanuck; directed by Walter Lang; screenplay by Ernest Pascal, based on the play by Maurice Maeterlinck. Filmed in Technicolor.

Shirley Temple, *Mytyl;* Spring Byington, *Mummy Tyl;* Nigel Bruce, *Mr. Luxury;* Gale Sondergaard, *Tylette the cat;* Eddie Collins, *Tylo the dog;* Johnny Russell, *Tyltyl.*

Some viewers and critics saw this Technicolor film (happiness is in your own backyard, not in fantasyland) based on a 1905 play as Fox's attempted answer to *The Wizard of Oz.* But it was deadly, in at least two senses of the word, and dated. Temple herself thought it was ahead of its time, and others thought so, too; in 1975 it was remade in Leningrad as the first U.S.–U.S.S.R. co-production, with Elizabeth Taylor, Jane Fonda, Cicely Tyson, Ava Gardner and others, directed by George Cukor. The Temple version, like its successor, lost money—her first film to do so.

Her fans couldn't accept Shirley as a brat—even a reformed one.

John Russell, Shirley Temple, Spring Byington and Russell Hicks were the Tyl family in *The Blue Bird.*

Sister and brother learn—with the help of Jessie Ralph as a good fairy and Helen Ericson as light (played in the 1975 re-make by Elizabeth Taylor) and their household pets—that the blue bird of happiness is at home, atfer all. Gail Sondergaard and Eddie Collins agree.

Tylo the Dog (Eddie Collins) and Ty-lette the Cat (Gale Sondergaard) eased Shirley's journey to fantasyland in *The Blue Bird,* but couldn't save the picture from becoming Shirley's first financial flop.

Shirley and Johnny Russell get a glimpse of luxury, and they like it.

YOUNG PEOPLE

1940; 20th Century-Fox, produced by Harry Joe Brown; directed by Allan Dwan; screenplay by Edwin Blum and Don Ettlinger; songs by Mack Gordon, Harry Warren (including "Strolling on the Avenue", "I Wouldn't Take a Million)."

Shirley Temple, *Wendy;* Jack Oakie, *Joe Ballentine;* Charlotte Greenwood, *Kit Ballentine;* George Montgomery, *Mike Shea;* Mae Marsh, *Marie Liggett;* Darryl Hickman, *Tommy.*

Young People not only took Shirley back to the familiar orphan-and-vaudeville-couple format, but under Dwan's direction it shamelessly used clips of musical numbers from her earlier films. The two new songs and her lively two new co-stars, Oakie and Greenwood, give *Young People* a certain sparkle, but its very title (as opposed to "children") is the tip-off. At twelve, Shirley was simply too old to be a cute child—and too young to be an interesting adolescent.

Jack Oakie was a loud-mouthed vaudeville partner and adoptive dad to Shirley in *Young People;* his breakfasts weren't bad either.

Charlotte Greenwood and Shirley sing to cheer up youngsters trapped in a farmhouse in New England during a hurricane.

Shirley sings "We're young people . . . we're not little babies anymore." Alas, she's so right.

213

The first time Shirley appeared on screen in an evening gown was in *Kathleen*. The gown was copied from the one she wore to her first Westlake School dance.

KATHLEEN

*1941;   Metro-Goldwyn-Mayer,   produced   by
George Haight; directed by Harold S. Bucquet;
screenplay by Mary C. McCall, Jr., based on the
story by Kay Van Riper.*

Shirley Temple, *Kathleen Davis;* Herbert Marshall,
John Davis; Laraine Day, *Dr. A. Martha Kent;* Gail
Patrick, *Lorraine Bennett.*

On *Kathlen's release,* Shirley's work in it was
praised ("an appealing young lady of quiet charm
and impressive assurance," wrote one national
reviewer), but her comeback movie for a new
studio came off as just another remake of *Poor
Little Rich Girl.* She played the miserable daughter
of a widower who neglects her. Psychologist-
companion Laraine Day arrives in the house, con-
verts Shirley to happiness and marries Daddy,
after getting rid of the gold-digging existing fiancee
Gail Patrick. A self-assured actress of thirteen,
Shirley seemed embarrassed by her banal script,
and cancelled her modest MGM contract with no
resistance from the studio.

'Ebony,' a French poodle who appeared in several scenes,
and Shirley rehearse on the *Kathleen* set.

Herbert Marshall scolds Shirley
for yet another nasty prank
played on her domineering
nurse.

215

As a psychologist, Laraine Day is hired to move in with, and take care of, Shirley, who has her doubts about the arrangement. But Laraine stays to become her stepmother.

Laraine Day tries to help Shirley understand her (once again) indifferent father.

216

Gail Patrick as "the other woman" is greeted icily by governess Laraine Day and Shirley as the daughter of the man Gail plans to marry. Shirley's reaction is to spill coffee on the golddigger's new spring outfit.

Joe Edmundson, Kathleen's sound man, gives Shirley a lesson between takes.

217

MISS ANNIE ROONEY

1944; David O. Selznick—United Artists; directed by John Cromwell; screenplay by Selznick, based on the novel by Margaret Buell Wilder.

Claudette Colbert, *Anne Hilton, mother;* Jennifer Jones, *Jane Hilton;* Joseph Cotten, *Lt. Anthony Willett;* Shirley Temple, *Bridget (Brig) Hilton;* Monty Wooley, *Col. Smollet;* Lionel Barrymore, *preacher;* Robert Walker, *Corp. William G. Smollet II;* Agnes Moorehead, *Emily Hawkins;* Hattie McDaniel, *Fidelia;* Guy Madison, *Harold Smith, sailor;* Craig Stevens, *Danny Williams;* Keenan Wynn, *Lt. Solomon;* Nazimova, *Zofia Kislowska, welder.*

The third time was the charm. Shirley breezed through the part of the mid-teen "Brig," Claudette Colbert's daughter and Jennifer Jones's kid sister in this Selznick wartime epic. "I knew all about her right from the beginning," said Shirley of Brig, "because she was practically me." The movie itself was sublime and Shirley's self-confidence gave her back a glow that had been too long missing from her performances. She worked well with Colbert, Jones and Monty Woolley (as the family's crusty lodger), and with Cotten and Robert Walker as young servicemen. Old friends and

The long tresses, high heels and lipstick of a typical wartime teenager were an unaccustomed sight to Temple fans—but welcome ones, as it turned out.

Monty Woolley, as the lodger, and Shirley move one family pet unlikely to steal scenes from the all-pro cast.

221

Walker and Jones, husband and wife in real life, and Temple and Colbert, were all splendid in their depictions of wartime concern and anguish.

In real life Shirley was sixteen and experimenting with more grown-up hairdos; in the movie her mother is ready to accept "Brig" without the pigtails.

We never see the soldier-father in *Since You Went Away*, but concern for his safety is the constant undercurrent in the movie.

222

Shirley and Jennifer Jones played sisters in the movie but were potential rivals for all the ingenue roles under the Selznick banner. Selznick not only chose Jones, letting Temple go on a series of loanouts, he later married her.

As "Brig," Shirley had several household chores; here she rests on her vacuum between takes.

The stars of *Since You Went Away* lined up in exact order of billing: Claudette Colbert, Joseph Cotten, Jennifer Jones, Shirley Temple, Monty Woolley, Lionel Barrymore, Robert Walker.

co-stars like Hattie McDaniel and Lionel Barrymore were on hand to help make the picture a happy experience. *Since You Went Away* was instantly popular and has remained a classic as a glimpse of the American homefront in World War II.

223

I'LL BE SEEING YOU

1944; David O. Selznick—United Artists; directed by William Dieterle; screenplay by Marion Parsonnet, based on the radio play by Charles Martin.

Ginger Rogers, *Mary Marshall;* Joseph Cotten, *Zachary Morgan;* Shirley Temple, *Barbara Marshall;* Spring Byington, *Mrs. Marshall;* Tom Tully, *Mr. Marshall;* Chill Wills, *Swanson.*

Quickly, Selznick cast Shirley in a lower budget but still stylish companion piece to *Since. You Went Away.* Again the setting was wartime, and again Cotten was the romantic male lead. Ginger Rogers played his romantic interest and Shirley played her younger cousin—and third lead this time. "I had a tremendous crush on Joseph Cotten," she recalled. "I thought he was just perfect. He had a charming manner, and he treated me as a sixteen-year-old should be treated—as an equal. I would be a little shy when I wasn't supposed to be. When he and Ginger announced that they were going to get married, I had to throw my arms around his neck. I remember it was very exciting at the time."

Although actually Ginger's cousin in this film, Shirley again played a "kid sister" kind of role—she spoiled things for a while by revealing Ginger's prison background.

Ginger and Shirley disagree with director Dore Shary's notion for this scene.

Shirley tried to cause trouble between Joseph Cotten and Ginger Rogers in *I'll Be Seeing You*. Spring Byington played her mother.

One of Shirley's teen crushes—on a man and his uniform—was Joseph Cotten, her co-star in *I'll Be Seeing You*.

Darryl Hickman chides Shirley, and Virginia Welles, for their failure to make a sale.

KISS AND TELL

1945; Columbia, produced by Sol Siegel; directed by Richard Wallace; screenplay by F. Hugh Herbert, based on his own play.

Shirley Temple, *Corliss Archer;* Jerome Courtland, *Dexter Franklin;* Walter Abel, *Mr. Archer;* Robert Benchley, *Uncle George;* Tom Tully, *Mr. Pringle;* Darryl Hickman, *Raymond Pringle.*

Kiss and Tell was the Corliss Archer story based on the hit Broadway play about three romantic but prankish teenagers and their feuding parents. As Corliss, the famous 1940s teenager Shirley would play once again, she won lavish praise from critics and instant box-office success. *Time's* usually caustic movie reviewer called her "a first-rate comedienne and a very attractive young lady [who] forgot none of the tricks that once made her the cinema's most dreaded scene thief."

In the movie script, Corliss Archer runs a USO charity bazaar stocked with hand-embroidered guest towels. Business is nonexistent until she persuades her boyfriend to buy five towels for five dollars. In gratitude she kisses him, and several servicemen standing by assume she is selling kisses and form a line. The scene required 150 atmosphere players or extras including twenty-two kissers who had their day pay rates adjusted upward for the "business" they were doing. The kissers were specially selected clean-cut young men, certified for their roles by a male nurse who took temperatures and sprayed their throats. (One boy was rejected for garlic on the breath.) Mrs. Temple naturally reserved the right of veto of any candidate but didn't exercise it.

Shirley, who had had real-life kissing experience only on such occasions as New Year's Eve, threw herself into the job. "Of course I'll kiss them on the mouth," she said. "That's the only kind of kisses worth paying for—kisses on the cheek are just gratuities." Her private philosophy, she allowed, was "a girl shouldn't kiss a boy the first time they're out together—despite the current speedup." Gertrude Temple, standing by as always, made her own observation: "I don't ordinarily get to see Shirley kissing. It is very interesting."

Jean Louis designed the junior miss fashions for Shirley in *Kiss and Tell*, including this blue checked gingham pinafore and oval-necked white organza blouse.

229

Having no luck selling towels at a bazaar for servicemen, Shirley switched to kisses, and threw herself into her work.

With Scott MacKay, Shirley played somewhat hard-to-get.

230

Jerome Courtland courted Shirley in *Kiss and Tell*, but it wasn't her towels he wanted, it was her lips.

Robert Benchley as a navy chaplain rehearsed Shirley as Corliss Archer for marriage to Jerome Courtland, in *Kiss And Tell*.

Shirley finally gets the right guy in the corner of the kitchen.

HONEYMOON

1947; RKO Radio; directed by William Keighley; screenplay by Michael Kanin, based on the story by Vicki Baum.

Shirley Temple, *Barbara Olmstead;* Franchot Tone, *David Flanner;* Guy Madison, *Phil Vaughn;* Lina Romay, *Raquel Mandoza;* Gene Lockhart, *Prescott.*

In *Honeymoon,* the perfect movie to watch on TV on a rainy Saturday afternoon, Shirley imagines herself to be in love with Franchot Tone, American vice-consul in Mexico City. Tone is trying to straighten out Shirley and her soldier-groom, Guy Madison.

The situations were less than hilarious, but Temple and Madison were a cute honeymoon couple.

Forgetting why she came to Mexico City (Guy Madison), Shirley makes a play for Franchot Tone.

Guy Madison and Shirley, who once dated in real life, were the hot-cha new romantic couple in *Honeymoon.*

Shirley removed some tell-tale lipstick (hers) from Franchot Tone's face in the four-sided romantic tangle, set in Mexico.

233

THE BACHELOR AND THE BOBBY SOXER

Shirley prepares Cary Grant for the potato sack race.

237

The future governor of California, Ronald Reagan, and his future candidate for Congress took their roles in *That Hagen Girl* very seriously.

THAT HAGEN GIRL

*1947; Warner Bros. produced by Alex Gottlieb;
directed by Peter Godfrey; screenplay by Charles
Hoffman, based on the novel by Edith Kneipple
Roberts.*

Shirley Temple, *Mary Hagen;* Ronald Reagan, *Tom
Bates;* Rory Calhoun, *Ken Freneau;* Conrad Janis,
Dewey Koons.

At age nineteen, Shirley made "my favorite
adult picture," *That Hagen Girl,* co-starring the
future governor of California and her later political ally, Ronald Reagan. The movie's story·line
was straight soap opera, but it did give her a
chance to act, and even to attempt to commit
suicide. (One cruel critic wrote that it was too bad
the attempt had failed.)

That Hagen Girl was the least typical and most dramatic
Temple movie.

In one of its lighter moments, Shirley danced with Rory
Calhoun.

In the late 1940s they were nobody's favorite actor and
actress, but in the late 1960s both made a big splash in
California politics.

239

FORT APACHE

1948; RKO Radio; directed by John Ford; screenplay by Frank Nugent, based on the novel "Massacre" by James Warner Bellah.

John Wayne, *Captain York*; Henry Fonda, *Col. Thursday*; Shirley Temple, *Philadelphia Thursday*; Pedro Armendariz, *Sgt. Beaufort*; John Agar, *Lt. O'Rourke*; Victor McLaglen, *Sgt. Mulachy*.

Shirley's old friend John Ford directed this horse opera, and her husband John Agar was co-starred with her for the first time. But neither of those things (nor John Wayne or Henry Fonda) could save the plot: her soldier father objects to her boyfriend, who becomes a hero by escaping from an Indian massacre and bringing news of it back to the fort.

With Irene Rich and Anna Lee.

241

Colonel Thursday (Henry Fonda) issues strict orders. With Ward Bond, Irene Rich, and John Agar.

Admonishing Captain York (John Wayne) as John Agar adds a reproving look.

Bad news or good? It's hard to tell. With Anna Lee and Irene Rich.

243

ADVENTURE IN BALTIMORE

1949; RKO Radio; directed by Richard Wallace, screenplay by Lionel Houser, based on a story by Christopher Isherwood and Lesser Samuels.

Robert Young, *Dr. Sheldon;* Shirley Temple, *Dinah Sheldon;* John Agar, *Tom Wade.*

This turn-of-the-century story had a pleasant look about it, and Robert Young was appealing as Shirley's minister-father. But Shirley as a social-political rebel (she lands in jail for crusading for women's suffrage) was unbelievable, and a third-billed John Agar was no help at all.

Shirley had eyes only for John Agar in their second film together; he still couldn't act, but their being together helped boost the box office, as it had with *Fort Apache.*

A Baltimore kitchen, circa 1908. Josephine Hutchinson lectures, but Shirley has a liberated mind of her own.

245

To go to college with Mr. Belvedere, Shirley sported a new, shorter, collegiate hair-do.

MR. BELVEDERE GOES TO COLLEGE

1949; 20th Century-Fox; directed by Elliott Nugent; screenplay by Richard Sale, Mary Loos and Mary McCall, Jr., based on characters created by Gwen Davenport.

Clifton Webb, *Lynn Belvedere*; Shirley Temple, *Ellen Baker*; Tom Drake, *Bill Chase*; Jessie Royce Landis, *Mrs. Chase.*

Without her old home studio's knowledge, Shirley was pregnant with her first child, Linda Susan, during the making of *Mr. Belvedere Goes to College.* "We wrote the script as we went along, and it was a good idea," she recalled in half-hearted defense. It was a terrible idea: a journalism student, desperate for a story, pursues Mr. Belevedere, who is publicity-shy.

Mr. Belvedere (Clifton Webb) went to college, and second-billed Shirley went along for the ride.

Seabiscuit, Shirley and Barry Fitzgerald were win, place and show in the racehorse's movie biography.

THE STORY OF SEABISCUIT

1949; Warner Bros.; directed by David Butler; screenplay by John Taintor Foote, based on his own story.

Shirley Temple, *Margaret O'Hara;* Barry Fitzgerald, *Shawn O'Hara;* Lon McCallister, *Ted Knowles;* Rosemary De Camp, *Mrs. Charles Howard.*

In this "biopic" about the famous race horse, Shirley co-starred with one of Seabiscuit's cousins. Her father trained horses and her fiance rode Seabiscuit into the winner's circle. She picked up an Irish brogue from Barry Fitzgerald, but rode the movie into the loser's circle.

Lon McCallister was Shirley's flame in *The Story of Seabiscuit,* but he loved his horse just about as much.

To play Barry Fitzgerald's daughter in *The Story of Seabiscuit* Shirley attempted an Irish brogue. It, she and the movie (her next-to-last) received unanimously disastrous reviews.

249

Taking care of Dad . . . with Virginia Welles, Nana Bryant, Tom Tully and Roy Roberts.

A KISS FOR CORLISS

1949; United Artists; directed by Richard Wallace; screenplay by Howard Dimsdale, based on characters created by F. Hugh Herbert.

Shirley Temple, *Corliss Archer;* David Niven, *Kenneth Marquis;* Tom Tully, *Harry Archer;* Darryl Hickman, *Dexter Franklin;* Virginia Welles, *Mildred;* Gloria Holden, *Mrs. Archer.*

In her very last feature film Shirley reprised her screen character from *Kiss and Tell,* but she was the first to admit "the result was not terribly good." Niven, who co-starred as a much older womanizer, went further and called it "a disastrous pot-boiler." The plot had Niven in the middle of his third divorce, with Harry Archer (Tom Tully) as the third wife's lawyer. To make her boyfriend Dexter jealous, Shirley, as Corliss, invents a romance with the Niven character, Kenneth Marquis, and fictionalizes the details of her romance in her diary. She makes sure that Dexter sees the diary, but when Marquis also does, he shows it to Mr. Archer and says that he will keep his "promise" and marry Corliss.

The movie's script was re-written several times to try to combat the Motion Picture Producer's Association's objections that it treated divorce too lightly. It remained a tasteless script, especially for Shirley, who was on the verge of her own divorce. Also as, a young mother, she shouldn't have tried to squeeze out one more bobby-soxer vehicle.

For such an uninteresting and unimportant film *A Kiss for Corliss* had a negative niche in movie history, at least for its principals. C.A. Lejune, writing in the London Sunday *Observer,* summed up the picture's critical response with a poem:

> *Sometimes I think that David Niven*
> *Should not take all the parts he's given.*
> *While of the art of Shirley Temple,*
> *I, for the moment, have had ample.*

David Niven asked for and got his release from his contract with Samuel Goldwyn (who had been trying to get him to quit anyway) after *A Kiss for Corliss.* Shirley decided that the public had had ample of her for good, settled her contract with Selznick, and retired forever from movies. She then turned to her mounting personal troubles. She was twenty-one years old.

With Darryl Hickman.

With Virginia Welles and Tom Tully.

252

A puzzled David Niven eyes his young friend while her father (Tom Tully) looks on.

Hiding out with Darryl Hickman.

253

In *Shirley Temple's Storybook*, Elsa Lanchester played Mother Goose to a real gaggle, and was supported by Rod McKuen (over her right shoulder) and Shirley herself, playing Polly to a real kettle.

THE SHIRLEY TEMPLE STORYBOOK

Sixteen shows were done, three live and thirteen on film. NBC's TV network sprang for the additional cost of doing the first show in color. Shirley had script approval (the teleplays were adapted from well-known fairy tales) and acted in three of the shows, doing the rest as hostess-narrator. Mack David and Jerry Livingston, who had written the music for Walt Disney's *Cinderella*, wrote "Dreams Are Made for Children," which Shirley sang to open and close the program, and the other music for the series. She was worried about how she'd sound as she hadn't sung—except for a bit for RKO that was cut into insignificance in a teen film—since she was eleven. As narrator she appeared in the opening shot of each show in a ball gown by Don Loper (none of the sixteen different ones—one for each show—cost less than $600) on a wool-decked platform designed to resemble a floating cloud, backed by eight chiffon draperies and two chandeliers. She sat on a movable bicycle seat hidden by her dress and anchored on a pole. A large fairy-tale book showed scenes from the stories.

Beauty and the Beast was chosen as the opening show because the story could be told on television almost identically to the original written fairytale already familiar to the viewing audience. Claire Bloom and Charlton Heston, near the beginnings of their careers, were hired to play the title parts, and E. G. Marshall played the merchant. Claire Bloom could hardly wait to meet the narrator and fascinatedly watched Shirley's rehearsals. "I loved her when I was a little girl," explained Claire; "I always called her Shirley Tempa." Five-and-a-half-year-old Charles Jr., a little cheekier when he heard the premiere program was *Beauty and the Beast*, said, "Gee, Mom, you'll make a nifty beast."

But Shirley's first acting in the storybook series came in a Dutch costume and a blonde wig as the flirtatious Katrina Van Tassel in *The Legend of Sleepy Hollow*. It took ten days to prepare for live telecasts. "Shirley learned her lines in two days," Alvin Cooperman, the associate producer, said, "and was ready for direction when she came down from Atherton for rehearsals." Shirley read all the scripts carefully—whether she was going to appear in them or not—and made suggestions for changes. In *Beauty and the Beast* she felt that Beauty did not change character enough as the show progressed. "So we did quite a lot of rewriting, and Shirley was right," said story editor Norman Lessing. "I didn't know she was really reading all that stuff," said producer Henry Jaffe. "We sent it to her as a matter of course. But not only did she read all the scripts, she also came up with some good ideas; I don't know whether they were intuitive or the products of her measured thinking, but they were always incisive. She had such good taste and such a sense of fitness of things that we consulted her on many things that didn't concern her."

Shirley carried out her hostess chores in a slightly babyish singsong voice, and a bit glassy-eyed for the small home screens. Jaffe and Cooperman were delighted, however. "She had all the warmth and laughter in her voice that the series needed," said Cooperman. "She was the storyteller telling stories to her children. Nobody could be better." Jaffe extolled: "There were unexplored depths in Shirley as an actress, dancer and singer. But to plumb those depths would take time, and Shirley didn't want to be tied up in her new career for more than a few days a month."

The sixteen shows, which were not shown on a regular night, but rather pre-empted different NBC shows during children's evening viewing hours, also included *Rumplestiltskin* live and *The Nightingale*, *Dick Whittington and His Cat*, *Hiawatha*, *Charlotte's Web* and *Son of Aladdin* on film. *Mother Goose*, starring Elsa Lanchester in the title role with Shirley as Polly Put-the-Kettle-on, was the grand Christmas 1958 spectacular show, and provided Susan, Charles Jr. and Lori Black with their first and only professional acting roles.

Shirley had taken each child singly to the filming of one of her shows to be sure each understood the need for her brief monthly absences in Hollywood. And Lori at three and a half had been quite put out at not being allowed to sing on the first Storybook show. But Shirley had been determined that her children not be exploited as professional actors, and none had shown any particular inclination towards acting, singing or dancing. When the family was still in the Washington area, Susan was cast as a fairy in a pre-Christmas school version of *Cinderella*. "I made her costume out of crepe paper and tinsel ribbon, and built gossamer wings," Shirley recalled. "I was amazed to learn that the school was selling tickets to the play in a public auditorium with the

255

promise of Susan's appearance in her stage debut. Off I marched to withdraw her from the school. I have no reason to regret my decision despite the wintry blast of publicity. I was not going to let her appear before four hundred people, nor let anyone commercialize on my daughter's presence."

Bits parts in "Mother Goose" for national television, under Mommy's watchful eye, were something else again. A stagehand said the word "shit" during rehearsal, and Shirley had him fired. "This is a show for children," she explained to a dumbfounded cast (that included a young Joel Grey as Jack of "Jack and Jill" and a young Rod McKuen as Simple Simon)—since no children, including hers, were present at the incident.

Even Mrs. Gertrude Temple made a return to stage motherdom on the occasion of her grandchildren's professional debuts and hovered about the set. The girls did their bits very well, but Charlie (as a young chap who climbs a lookout pole and says "Here comes Jack, here comes Jack") was wooden. The director asked him to repeat his line, which Charlies did with only slightly more animation. He was given a pathetic forced round of applause, led by his mother, for his second try. After "Shirley Temple's Storybook" went off the air in 1960, none of the Charles Black family of San Mateo County, California, made a living at acting.

Mrs. Black and Charles Jr., Susan and Lori prepare for the series by reading Japanese . . .

. . . and French fairy tales.

256